A
PENNINE PIONEER
BY
ALLEN HOLT

Summit tunnel in the golden age of steam (from an original painting by Tom Valentine)

A PENNINE PIONEER

THE HISTORY OF
SUMMIT RAILWAY TUNNEL

ALLEN HOLT

GEORGE KELSALL

**TO
DOROTHY ELIZABETH**

Printed by RAP
201 Spotland Road
Rochdale
OL12 7AF

Published by George Kelsall
22 Church Street
Littleborough
Lancashire
OL15 9AA

ISBN 0 946571 29 5

FOREWORD

Built during the first, and minor of the two Railway Manias, the Manchester & Leeds was from its inception overshadowed by a far bolder project – The Great Western Railway.

When that most consummate of engineers Isambard Kingdom Brunel, 1806–59, the builder of that prestigious line, turned his formidable attention towards railways he decided to rewrite history. Condemning out of hand all Stephenson type railways as mere "coal train lines", the young engineers fertile brain was brimming over with ideas and innovations he alone was convinced would revolutionise rail travel. First he widened the track gauge adopted by George Stephenson from 4ft 8½ in to 7ft the older engineer was understandably absolutely furious. That a mere *parvenu* should have the audacity to meddle in what he held as sacrosanct was intolerable – but that was only the beginning.

During the period in which British Rail invited tenders to build its new generation Intercity 250 class 155 mph express trains, one suspects they would have much preferred Brunel to have prevailed in the "Battle of the Gauges". A pro-position that was never on the cards, and yet, had Brunel begun his railway career a little earlier the whole course of British railway history just might have been transformed.

As the work of building the GWR got underway it very soon became apparent this line differed in every department from other railways. with its broad-gauge track, huge locomotives, luxuriant clerestory roofed carriages, and Italianate stations it straightway created a following bordering on near veneration. That interest having prevailed undiminished over the passing years, the line achieved cult status as – God's Wonderful Railway. It was against this impressive scenario George Stephenson set about building the first trans-Pennine railway, interest in which appears to have been solely a northern preoccupation. An unfortunate error of omission considering that within 5 years of its completion the Manchester & Leeds Railway notched up a remarkable succession of achievements commencing with;

A FISTFUL OF FIRSTS

(1) It was the first trans-Pennine railway to be built

(2) When opened in 1841 Summit tunnel was the longest railway tunnel in the world

(3) At its Miles Platting works in 1846 the M&L was the first railway company in the world to build its own locomotives

(4) The world famous Edmondson railway ticketing system was perfected on this line

(5) When opened in 1844 Victoria station, Manchester, was the largest in the country, and first to be named after a ruling monarch

Enlarged by numerous additions, take overs, and operating under a new name – The Lancashire & Yorkshire Railway Company, George Stephenson's indomitable line of easy gradients continued to chalk up firsts long after Brunel's broad-gauge was torn up. In its heyday the L&Y Rly. Co. carried more freight than any other railway company, and for a time operated the largest fleet of railway owned steamships from four ports; Liverpool, Fleetwood, Hull, and Goole. The company was again in the vanguard when a centralised control system, installed at Victoria station, monitored the movement of every train. And, shared a joint first in suburban electrification with the North Eastern Railway when its Liverpool – Southport service was converted.

In more recent times, when No 11 platform at Victoria station was connected to No 3 of Exchange station Manchester, at 2,238ft it became the longest station platform in Europe. Its Werneth incline on the original M&L branch line into Oldham, was until its closure on 7 January 1963, the steepest railway gradient operating a regular passenger service in the country. And finally, the great Summit tunnel fire of December 1984, scored yet another *dubious* first, as the worst ever tunnel fire in British railway history.

To avoid confusion arising from two very different numbering systems used to identify the air shafts at Summit tunnel. The list consisting of letter and numbers, dating from the very beginning of the great undertaking, is the one used throughout this history. These figures are easily updated to British Rail listing by referring to sectional tunnel drawing (r).

During the year in which George Stephenson's trans-Pennine masterpiece attained its sesquicentennial anniversary, there was to be no foreseeable impediment to mar a bicentennial celebration in 2041. Having survived two World Wars, Beeching, recession, and fire, with a track record second to none, this superlative ironroad of imperishable impressions rightly deserves its place in history as – A PENNINE PIONEER.

ROCHDALE 1999   **ALLEN HOLT**

CONTENTS

LIST OF ILLUSTRATIONS

1. IN THE BEGINNING

The idea of a trans-Pennine railway connecting the cities of Manchester and Leeds was first promulgated in 1825. Its promoters, a group of gentlemen, millowners, bankers, and exporters, formed themselves into a committee to consider the feasibility of such an enterprise. None was then a director for at that stage no capital had been raised.

All were extremely critical of canal companies, in particular they accused those in west Lancashire of combining to operate a monopolistic service through to the port of Liverpool. A service they considered to be slow and far too expensive for the conveyance of raw materials from, and marketable produce to, the great Port.

Charles Hadfield, the doyen of inland waterways, described the network of canals in England as being, "The Arteries of the Revolution". That they had been the lifeline of a burgeoning Industrial Revolution during the last quarter of the eighteenth century remains undisputed. By the 1820s they were impeding its progress as that great Revolution gathered momentum. The canal companies countered by arguing that reliability was far more important than speed, at the same time covering all their options by operating an express or flyboat service. Running to fixed timetables using relays of fresh horses, changes of crew, and operating twenty-four hours a day with priority given over all other craft on the navigation, the flyboat service carried a surcharge of twenty-five per cent. But it was all too late and far too expensive. It proved a damning indictment of west Lancashire's inland waterways inefficiency when Lancashire millowners complained that it often took longer to deliver bales of American cotton from Liverpool docks to their mills, than the time taken to cross the Atlantic under sail.

The 1825 trans-Pennine railway committee had been greatly influenced by events at Stockton and Darlington during that same year. Fortunately their enthusiasm had been tempered by severely depressed trading conditions prevailing, and they held back. With the benefit of hindsight they very soon realised what handicaps must undoubtedly have ensued had they gone forward with the venture at that time. Always assuming the necessary capital could have been raised, which seems highly unlikely. To simply transfer the limited technology used on the Stockton & Darlington Rly. into the Calder Valley would have been the height of folly. With its odd assortment of locomotive, rope, and horse traction, it pointed the way forward but was not the harbinger of a true railway era. Another five years were to elapse before *Rocket* the rightful prognosticator of that momentous event set forth full steam ahead to change the world.

A. *Early Pennine lines – first proposals*

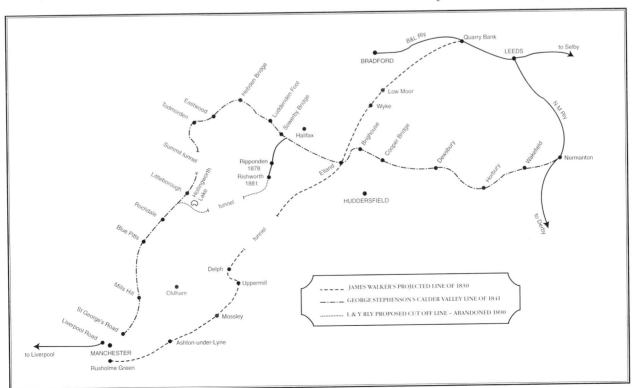

Within a matter of days prior to the grand opening of the Liverpool and Manchester Rly., on 15 September 1830, the trans-Pennine cadre met again to consider and clarify its position. It very quickly decided the time was now right to promote their project by convening a public meeting in Manchester on 18 October. There, before a "large and highly respectable meeting of the opulent classes of the district" the Manchester & Leeds Railway Company was formally constituted, with share-capital fixed at £800,000 in £100 shares. The Board was formulated to represent the interests of important places affected by the new line consisted of 29 directors; 10 from Manchester, 8 Leeds, 4 Liverpool, 3 Halifax, 2 Bradford, and 2 Rochdale. Two engineers – George Stephenson and James Walker — were appointed, and instructed to independently survey the most advantageous route through the Pennine hills.

When Walker arrived in Leeds he was informed by a firm of solicitors acting for the Company that Mr. Stephenson was working in the Calder Valley. Thus deprived of the easier option Walker's proposed line, see map (a) used Rusholme as its temporary Manchester terminus. The Board considered it to be "convenient for communicating with Manchester and the Liverpool and Manchester Railway" (sic). From there it was to proceed to a point just north of Ashton-under-Lyne, then north-eastwards skirting the sloping ground near Mossley, Uppermill, Dobcross to Delph, from where the line would pass along Broadhead Dale before entering a long tunnel. Emerging into the Dean Head Valley, then on towards Elland from where the line was drawn to cross the Vale of Calder near Brighouse, thence via Wyke, Low Moor, Bierley Chapel to Quarry Gap where it would connect with the Leeds – Bradford Railway at a distance of 7 miles from Leeds.

The M&L Board of Directors must have viewed with some dismay the prospect of having to build a long tunnel, thought to be well in excess of four miles long through difficult country, added to which, Walker in his report dated 3 November 1830, stated "...to avoid the use of inclined planes, deep and expensive cuttings would be unavoidable to maintain workable gradients". Had James Walker's imaginative but costly line been adopted, it would have reduced the M&L Rly. route mileage from 60 miles as built to 46 miles.

The Calder Valley line was truncated by degrees over a considerable length of time, the first cut came when running powers were obtained over a section of new line from Thornhill Junction into Leeds via Dewsbury, Batley, and the Morley tunnel 3369yd in 1848. Six-years later, an even more direct link was achieved by the sweeping curve of Hawkshaw's main line cut off at Milner Royd Junction, near Sowerby Bridge. Crossing the Calder Valley on the multi-arched Copley viaduct, the new line passed through Dryclough Junction to Halifax, Wyke, Low Moor, the Bowling tunnel 1648yd, Laisterdyke, Stanningly into Leeds, lopping a good 12 miles off George Stephenson's route. Shades of James Walker's proposed line here.

The third and final attempt at improving the lines circuitous route through the Calder Valley was both spectacular and unsuccessful. From an east facing junction built into the complex of the second Sowerby Bridge railway station, the cut off line was carried up the Valley of the Ryburn through Triangle to Ripponden by 1878, three years later it was extended to Rishworth. From there a proposed tunnel some 4 miles in length was to carry the line under Blackstone Edge, to emerge into Longden End Valley. After skirting Hollingworth Lake it would rejoin the main line near Clegg Hall, between Smithybridge and Rochdale.

Having climbed 233ft in a little under 3¾ miles between Sowerby Bridge and Rishworth the new line had gradients averaging 1 in 77.25 – unworkable in Stephenson's day except as inclined planes. Built to main line standards it included a 593ft tunnel, enormous retaining walls rising almost 90ft above the river, and a deep cutting. Many slips occurred delaying the opening of this short section of line which not unexpectedly cost a small fortune to build. The Company, beset with other more pressing commitments on its limited resources, was unable to justify the huge capital outlay of a second Pennine tunnel, and halted the project at Rishworth, temporarily.

In 1882 the promulgation of a new railway between Liverpool and Leeds by a group of prominent entrepreneurial gentlemen from Lancashire, came as a profound shock to the L&Y Rly. Co. To be styled the Yorkshire & Lancashire Railway & Tramway Company, preliminary surveys showed it to be considerably shorter, and in consequence much faster than the meandering Calder Valley line. Alarmed at the prospect of losing its monopoly the L&Y Rly. directors ordered an immediate new survey of its Rishworth – Smithybridge cut off scheme. The following newspaper report of that survey appeared on 21 October 1882.

Halifax Courier & Guardian
Local News page 4, col 5
Halifax

The surveys for the necessary plans to apply for powers to construct a line from Rishworth to Lancashire, by Blackstone Edge are just completed. The line extends from Slithero Bottom, along Blackstone Valley, and under the hill by tunnel, four miles in length, emerging near Hollingworth and skirting the Lake in the direction of Smithybridge and from thence to Rochdale. The route will thus run up a double line to Manchester and Liverpool, and will shorten the distance from Halifax to Rochdale by about five miles.

Both railway companies appear to have adopted a wait-and-see policy before committing themselves. The L&Y Rly. Co. decided to hold back with its cut off scheme until the proposed Yorkshire & Lancashire Railway & Tramway Company showed its hand in a more positive manner. The latter fearing the L&Y would go ahead and build the Blackstone Edge tunnel likewise procrastinated, an inglorious deadlock resulted in the abandonment of both undertakings.

The vast sums expended on the scenic Ryburn track as it climbed towards the Pennine hills it failed to penetrate were never recovered. As the main line it would have been truly inspiring, as a branch line it was an expensive failure, losing its skeletal passenger service earlier than most in 1929, all goods traffic had been withdrawn by 1958. The entire line, a lost cause to what might have been, was dismantled in 1962.

Had the L&Y Rly. Co. gone ahead with its inspired cut off scheme one can but speculate as to the extent of any social, political, or economic decline in towns and villages of the upper Calder Valley – Luddenden Foot, Hebden Bridge, Todmorden, Walsden and coupled with the closure of Summit tunnel – Littleborough, all demoted to branch line status. The knock-on effect would have had a malign influence on commerce in every one of those places. And, in more recent times how would the Hollingworth Lake Country Park have coped with a main line railway thundering through it? Who can doubt that a Lakeside railway station would have been a predictable development, bringing even bigger crowds "t' Weighver's Seaport".

THE ELEVEN TOWNS RAILWAY

But we digress, the year is 1830 and George Stephenson is at work in the Calder Valley. Unlike Walker's grandiose Pennine "up-and-under" G S followed the Rochdale Canal and River Calder around the hills, achieving a line of easy gradients well within the capacity of the tiny 80hp locomotives first used on the line. His was to be the first and best engineered line through the Pennines.

The engineer's proposals were approved without dissent by the Board, but only as far as Sowerby Bridge, from where they were unable to agree on the most advantageous route forward into Leeds. As they pondered it is quite reasonable to assume that the section of Walker's route through Wyke and Low Moor came under close scrutiny, or was it just coincidence they ground to a halt at Sowerby Bridge? At any rate the Board resolved the impasse, by deciding that an application for an Act of Parliament to build the new line from St George's Fields, Manchester citing Sowerby Bridge as its temporary eastern terminus, should be petitioned for forthwith.

The Bill was first introduced into the House of Commons on 10 March 1831, where, despite fierce opposition from the Rochdale Canal Company it received its first and second readings. Unfortunately the dissolution of Parliament on 23 April stopped any further progress. The directors petitioned for their Bill to be reintroduced in the ensuing session of Parliament, which was approved. By 2 June the Bill was committed for a second time, but on 12 July a Parliamentary Committee by a vote of 15 to 13 declared; "the preamble for an Act of Parliament to build a railway between Manchester and Leeds had not been proved," the Bill was thrown out. On 18 July the Board applied to the House for leave to have the Bill reconsidered by a Committee of Appeal, which was also granted. The Committee reported back on 28 July that it upheld the decision of the House, the Bill was abandoned. The Manchester & Leeds Railway was having a difficult birth.

Five more years were to elapse before any further progress was made, by which time the route into Leeds had been determined. It was to proceed from Sowerby Bridge along the Vale of Calder via Elland, Brighouse, Mirfield, Dewsbury, Horbury, Wakefield, and Normanton, see map (b) overleaf.

During February 1836 the whole parliamentary process started once again, and despite continued

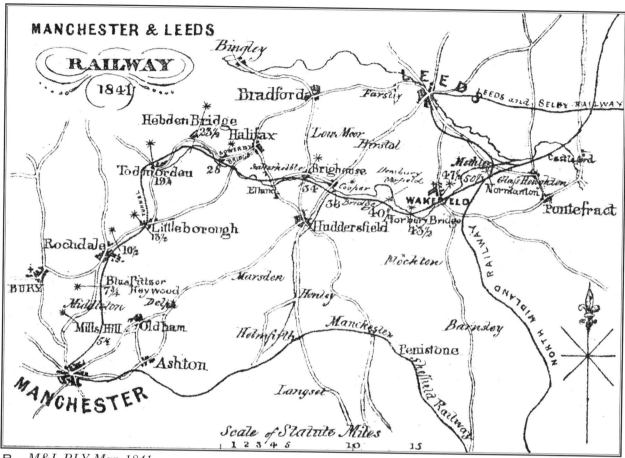

B – *M&L RLY Map 1841*

opposition from canal companies and landowners, on this occasion the Bill was successful. The royal assent being given to the Act of 6 and 7 William IV, chapter iii, on 4 July 1836, which authorised the Manchester & Leeds Rly. Co. to build its line. The North Midland Railway Company was under construction between Derby and Leeds at this time, and had already laid down a line of rails between Normanton and Leeds. By section 290 of its Act, M&L Rly. Co. was granted running powers on the North Midland rails for the remaining nine-miles into Leeds. In a reference to the new lines winding course through the industrial belts of Lancashire and Yorkshire, Edwin Butterworth of Oldham wrote:

> ... That because of its serpentine character and almost unrivalled means of access to such an unusual number of large and flourishing towns, that it might not be more aptly designated – The Eleven Towns Railway

Butterworth's "Eleven Towns" quip failed to note that quite a number of those flourishing towns were bypassed, some only partially, others totally; Huddersfield was 3¾ miles from the main line! The West Riding, heartland of Yorkshire's woollen industry, was severely affected by these omissions. A situation that could only be remedied by a proliferation of branch lines, requests for which the M&L was inundated with even before the main line opened. Nevertheless, the lines circuitous route proved to be its salvation, with the 1841 census showing that almost one million people lived and worked within 3 and 1,619,158 within 10 miles of the line, its potential was enormous.

There were two good reasons why George Stephenson's lack of any formal education did not inhibit the relentless progress he made towards perfecting steam locomotion. First was a restless inquiring mind that sought to solve the unsolvable – having expended an inordinate amount of time and energy trying to build a perpetual motion machine, he succeeded only in demonstrating his will and potential to succeed. Secondly an effusive degree of paternalism towards his only surviving offspring Robert (a daughter died in infancy) proved to be double-edged. The engineer, painfully aware of his own scholastic inadequacies saw to it that his son and heir received a good all-round education. In consequence of which he himself attained an acceptable standard of comprehension, by studying alongside his progeny at home.

Unfettered by the illiteracy and innumeracy that had dogged his youth George Stephenson then set his sights on distant horizons.While still working in the Tyneside Coalfields, long before his name became synonymous with railways, he once told Robert Summerside, an old and revered colleague, "...I will do something in coming time which will astonish all England".

When Robert Stephenson attended Edinburgh University as a bursar student of geology – his father provided the endowment, and would have been an avid reader of his son's books and field notes. Thus acquiring valuable knowledge that would have stood him in good stead when deliberating how best to put the new line through the Summit Pass.

In his *Geology of Burnley Coalfield* 1875 Professor Hall describes the Walsden Gorge, of which the Summit Pass is an integral part, as being "...one of the deepest and most perfectly formed in Lancashire". Just how it was formed and subsequently developed at the southern approach into the Pass is described in the following.

Summit

Portrait of a Village

As the last ice age came to a protracted close 10,000 years ago, temperatures began to rise causing the melting ice to form glacier lakes in valleys indented into the western slopes of the Pennines. And at a much later stage on the Lowlands of the west Lancashire Plain. Some, but by no means all, overflowed across Pennine watersheds creating new valleys and gorges, or reshaping existing ones.

Two south Pennine meltwater spillways, ground out by ice and deepened by water, united to fashion the Summit Pass, Walsden Gorge, and the Calder Valley. Aligning them into a continuous albeit winding communication channel through the Pennine hills. Where in the fullness of time George Stephenson would build the first trans-Pennine railway.

The northernmost of these channels was fed by a chain of interconnected glacier lakes in the Hurstwood, Swinden and Thursden valleys east of Burnley, which overflowed into an existing geological fault – Cliviger Gorge. For a considerable length of time the northern entrance to the Gorge remained blocked by an immense ice dam, which the escaping meltwater bypassed by flowing at high-level from Hurstwood into Catridge Clough, from where the water entered the Cliviger Gorge at Portsmouth, near Cornholme.

At about the same time deflected meltwater from Upper Rossendale flowed into the Rossendale and Irwell Valleys forming a large irregular shaped glacier lake which in turn overflowed into the Roch Valley. There, an enormous triangular shaped glacier lake with a surface area of 12 square miles was formed. Impounded by the ice sheet and the then unbreached south Pennine hills this rapidly filling lake eventually overflowed at the Summit watershed near Littleborough. The deluge of floodwater narrowed as the winding defile deepened to reshape the landscape into the Summit Pass and Walsden Gorge. It was the last, most important, and at 600ft OD the lowest of all Pennine meltwater spillways.

At Todmorden the two spillways merged before the floodwater surged on eastward through the Calder Valley, to spend its force in the Humber Estuary and North Sea. Long after the Roch Valley glacier lake ceased discharging into the Summit Pass – as the ice sheet receded its waters were diverted southwards to flow into the River Trent – the Cliviger Gorge continued to function as a meltwater spillway. Its great ice dam having been swept away the Hurstwood meltwater then entered the Gorge at its northern extremity.

The last period of glaciation had afforded Todmorden a unique bonus, scouring action of water turbulence at the confluence of the two meltwater spillways shaped a spectacular linear amphitheatre – the now densely wooded and truly magnificent, Centre Vale Park.

During the immediate postglacial period the Summit Pass was covered by a dwarf tundral vegetation of lichen and mosses. These in turn were replaced by trees tolerant of excess moisture – Hazel, Alder, Willow, and Birch, transforming the Pass into a "carr" type woodland. Later came the natural Oak, Elm, Ash, and Fir, completing the afforestation.

The floor of the steep sided U shaped valley was a waterlogged morass fed by brook and rivulet, headwaters of the Calder brook a tributary of the Yorkshire Calder and the Lancashire Roch. Cascading down through wooded cloughs on opposite hillsides, one flowing eastwards into the North Sea the other westward to the Irish Sea.

Sited against the high Pennines, a sublime backdrop for happenings long since gone, the wet brown reeded Pass remained a natural habitat for countless generations of waders and visiting wildfowl. The surrounding hills then canopied by sparse woodlands of hardy birch trees, which along with underlying herbage provided a modicum of covert refuge for wild boar and deer, all unseen by human eye. Neolithic man first appeared on the Pennies 8,000 years ago not to settle, but as bands of nomadic hunters ranging the hilltops in search of prey. Where continual discoveries of flints and arrowheads bear silent witness to their primitive existence. Scattered about on the Mesolithic floor level beneath accumulations of peat at around the 1,200 ft contour line, the artefacts of our feral ancestors are occasionally washed out after periods of heavy rain, exposed to the keen eyed.

The first settlers to leave more tangible evidence in the enclosed valley were the Celts, in 1832 a Late Celtic bronze torque of exquisite workmanship was unearthed at Mawrode (now debased to Moor Road) near Summit Village. In his book *The Roof of Lancashire* Herbert C Collins, draws the interesting analogy that mawr as in Mawrode is as inherently Celtic in origin as Penmaenmawr. Also derivation of the word Calder is Celtic for "a rapid stream". Other races came and went, but of all the early denizens it was the Saxons who left the most indelible mark. At the southern approach to the Pass at Littleborough, Ton House, now known as Townhouse is the fourth building to stand on the site of an authenticated Saxon settlement, and within the Pass there is an abundance of good old Anglo-Saxon place names.

After the Norman Conquest the first Manor Houses began to appear, followed during the thirteenth and fourteenth centuries by the founding of the Great Halls. By mid-seventeenth century a scatter of farmsteads were built on high ground above and overlooking the Pass, these were interconnected by packhorse tracks, one of which crossed the miry valley as best it could on stepping-stones. The first farmers were yeomen or common freeholders who, far from being self-sufficient eked out a precarious existence,

employing the distaff side of the family spinning yarn. If the output was of sufficient quantity a loom would be operated, the combined product of at least eight spinning wheels being required to keep one hand-loom weaver fully employed.

Implementation of the General Enclosures Acts, resulted in much larger parcels of farmland being defined by the omnipresent dry-stone walls, forcing many farmers to sell their holdings and become tenant farmers. None could have had any comprehension of the epoch making times to come at the dawn of the Industrial Revolution.

By an unpredictable quirk mother nature had fashioned a characteristic landscape at Summit, where the topography, geology, and climate, rendered it inexorably linked with transport and manufacturing. Circumstances that influenced later generations of landowning farmers to give up the unremitting life of hill farming, when they became inspired by a more lucrative idea. Appreciating the economic significance of their holdings they worked the mineral wealth beneath the land to fuel the new dynamic industrial age. The landscape became scarred as delphs, stone quarries, brickmaking, and drift mining enterprises got underway – the devastation of a once idyllic defile had begun.

The first transport development designed specifically for wheeled conveyance came in 1796 when a turnpike-road advanced cautiously along the valley floor from the direction of Walsden. But at the Steanor Bottom Toll Bar had to climb higher ground through Dog Isles, and Calderbrook village to avoid quagmire. Two years later the first section of the Rochdale Canal opened between Sowerby Bridge and Rochdale, passing through the Summit coomb in fine style along a lengthy summit pound. Which inadvertently gave the name Summit to an area previously annexed by Calderbrook, and in earlier times was known as Wilderness.

The still waters of the navigation did nothing to detract from the beauty of the verdant valley, indeed, according to one eyewitness it was if anything greatly enhanced by it. The anonymous writer, a passenger travelling by stagecoach along the top road through Calderbrook village in 1805, looking down into the Pass he wrote "...the shaded streams of the meandering river and the artful lines of the navigation are pleasant guides through this charming glen". Now denuded of much of its tree life it is an area of stark contrasts, a lush green valley floor and millstone-grit outcrops silhouetted against the skyline 300 ft above. It will become more colourful when the waterway is reopened to pleasure craft in the not too distant future. Now within sight of its bicentenary the connected eastern section is being painstakingly restored by bands of dedicated enthusiasts. At the time of writing joiners from the Calderdale Canal Restoration Team and Rochdale MBC Direct Works Dept. are replacing missing lock gates in the Pass. Industry too is making valuable contributions towards this work, Courtaulds having paid for the restoration of Punchbowl Lock in Summit Village.

The new waterway also did something else intrinsically beneficial to Summit, as the canal wended its way through the district it served as a huge drain, channelling surplus surface water out of the Pass. Slowly but surely the valley bottom wetlands began to dry out, enabling an extension of the turnpike-road forward from Steanor Bottom Toll Bar to Littleborough by 1824. Almost immediately the first houses were built, setting out the site of the new village. Aligned along both sides of the new thoroughfare all were sturdily built in local squared stone,

1. *Summit village from Temple Lane, showing airshafts No 1½ and No 2*

Considering that the Rochdale Canal was of necessity so very heavily locked – there were ninety-two in all, commercially it was by far and away the most successful of the three trans-Pennine waterways. The calculated effect on intercounty trade was both immediate and lasting, in the wider context of export markets the cock-a-hoop proprietors proudly proclaimed they had "Joined the Irish Sea to the German Ocean". Which they had, for the Rochdale formed the missing link in a network of inland waterways linking the Ports of Liverpool and Hull. American raw cotton arriving from the west was after manufacture exported into Europe through the Port of Hull, conversely Yorkshire woollen goods were exported to North America via Liverpool.

some in vernacular style of building had long-light windows to upper storeyed weaving chambers. Religious fervour amongst the pioneer villagers resulted in a number of places of worship being built. All were of formal appearance and strictly utilitarian of purpose, to serve the dissenting factions for Summit was, and still is, a Chapel village. It was all a far cry from the humiliation their forebears suffered at the hand of the Revd. William Grimshaw, Rector of Haworth Parsonage. Following a visit he made into the Pass during 1747 the controversial clergyman asserted that he had "...introduced the preaching into a dark and ignorant part of Lancashire called Deanhead". Two years later John Wesley arrived on horseback preaching outdoors to converts of the Methodist cause.

If public houses and ecclesiastical buildings are seen by some to form an unholy alliance when sited in close proximity, it should perhaps be noted that both form a fundamental part in the social fabric of urbanisation however large or small the development. It was therefore not all that surprising when James Lord 1790 – 1869 owner of the Bull and Butcher alehouse, at Dog Isles on the top road decided to move. Having lost most of his passing trade due to the turnpike diversion, he dismantled the property stone by stone and re-erected it on a prime site – at the head of the new village, not all that far from where the first Chapel was built.

As one of the leading lights in the community James Lord aptly renamed his establishment the Summit Inn (2). It was destined to become the hostelry most frequented by railway personnel during the period 1837-41, serving severally as; A banqueting-hall where M&L directors entertained important visitors to the tunnel – as a coroners court where, the Rochdale Coroner held inquests over the bodies of men and boys killed in the tunnel – as a wages office, where on alternate Saturday teatimes the tunnel contractor paid his men their dues, when not unexpectedly the Inn became a venue for a railway navvies drunken orgy. The Inn also doubled as the village barber shop, a service few navvies availed themselves of, for a good shock of hair was the key to regular employment, proving beyond all doubt the hirsute applicant had not recently been incarcerated in HM prison.

2. *The Summit Inn – inexorable link with early railway history*

But before all that, for a brief seventeen-years Summit enjoyed the rural simplicity of a typical Pennine "one street village". A place where silent boats passed serenely and silently along shallow gliding waters of its navigation through the silvan Pass. A tranquil place, disturbed only by the lowing herd, the daily clatter of hand-loom weaving and strident notes of posthorns as the Leeds – Manchester stage coaches *Perserverance* and *Shuttle* rattled along its winding street twice weekly.

That peace ended abruptly with arrival of steam power and its attendant factory system of manufacturing. The fact that stationary and locomotive steam-engines were introduced almost simultaneously at Summit, shows it was by no means first in the field, on the other hand the new source of energy was adopted with enthusiasm. Before the coming of the railway a Mr Hudson owned and operated a print shop at Gale. In its wake the first purpose-built cotton mill was built at Green Vale, and Burgess & Townsend opened their print and dye works in Smithy Nook about the same time.

These were followed in fairly rapid succession by others whose workforce did not reside in the village but walked to work from surrounding moorland farms and hamlets. As the factory system spread a proliferation of Summit's housing stock, built to accommodate the growing numbers of mill workers, took place. Making maximum use of the narrow valley floor terraced houses were juxtaposed in short narrow side streets.

By the mid-nineteenth century Summit had assumed the guise of yet another unlovely but workmanlike textile village, complete with an obligatory pall of sulphurous smoke. Consolidation of the textile industry during the reign of King Cotton meant full employment and an increase in the living standards of his legionary workers. It was a true measure of Lancashire's industrial might that; on any one working day enough cloth was produced in its mills before breakfast to clothe the nation, the rest of the days output was for export. It was also a time when little or no thought was given to the havoc wrought in the countryside. As technological advancement trebled production overworked mill engines poured out clouds of poisonous black smoke, polluting the air with soot and grime, giving rise to the euphemism – even the sparrows cough in Lancashire!

Perhaps the millowners honestly believed that industry and the environment could coexist at no extra cost to themselves.

In that respect at least Summit was more

fortunate than most industrialised areas. The arrival in the village of the textile firm Fothergill & Harvey (founded 1848) during 1859 marked the beginning of a long and meaningful association with the Harvey family, and with Alexander Gordon Cummins Harvey, 1858 – 1922 in particular. Gordon Harvey, as he was affectionately known by all who knew him, was a genial liberal minded Liberal of the first order, a man whose generosity and kindness will long be remembered. In 1879, at the tender age of twenty-one he was appointed works manager at the Sladen Wood Mill, Summit, where he very quickly set about improving the lot of his impoverished workers. Hot drinks awaited children as they arrived at the mill half-starved on cold winter mornings, canteen and recreational facilities were provided long before other industrialists acquiesced to such extravagances. By the turn of the century Gordon Harvey, then head of the firm, had begun to build houses for Fothergill & Harvey workers at Timbercliffe and Deanhead, the later being the one and only conscious attempt ever made to extend Summit village northward into the Pass. Although a number of houses were built at Deanhead betwixt road and canal, the original scheme which included retirement homes for long service employees, was curtailed by the outbreak of hostilities in 1914.

The wealthy Harvey family lived at Townhouse a large edifice standing in rural surrounding on the outskirts of Littleborough, (previously referred to in this chapter) it was originally the ancestral home of the Newalls. As an industrialist, politician, and environmentalist. Harvey was again in the vanguard, when at his behest emission of smoke at all his mills was eliminated, by converting the boilers to consume smoke. A course of action he pursued with some vigour when elected Member of Parliament for Rochdale in 1906. His campaign resulted in Harvey's Smoke Abatement Bill of 1912. Which would

compel "...every furnace or fireplace, other than domestic, to be constructed or altered so as to consume smoke", unfortunately the Bill was lost on a guillotine motion. The aspirations of the Member for Rochdale had to wait a further 44 years when the Clean Air Act of 1956 heralded the start of Smokeless Zones ending atmospheric pollution. A G C Harvey was a reformist whose philanthropic work at Summit pointed the way forward towards a better and brighter future.

This then was the village George Stephenson visited between 1829-41, although no reliable record comes down to us as to the frequency of those visits, they were numerous. He came on horseback, by carriage, and eventually by the railway he built.

Vestiges of the embryonic village the engineer knew so well exist aplenty, despite recent attempts at improving it! The Summit Inn still stands foursquare sentinel of the Pass, and ought to have a Stephenson Bar or Room, he was after all the inns most famous customer. Also at the top end of the village is the first chapel of 1834, now in a state of dereliction, nearby is the Royal Oak – renamed The Huntsman Hotel in 1962. Some of the original ribbon development built to house the hand-loom weavers is still there, as is the flight of stone steps climbing out of the deep cutting he used so often. But paramount in this link with the past is the great tunnel which put this tiny village well and truly on the map.

A tunnel George Stephenson never really wanted to build, in fact against his better judgement he openly stated on two occasions it would not be necessary. It was his subordinate Thomas Longridge Gooch who, after no fewer than five detailed surveys, proved beyond all doubt that a long and expensive tunnel at Summit was the only way this Pennine Pioneer Railway could traverse the foothills of the high Pennines.

2. Lines to Littleborough

They plunge through the bowels of mountains they undertake to drain lakes; they bridge valleys with viaducts; their steepest gradients are gentle undulations; their curves are lines of beauty; they interrupt no traffic; they touch no prejudice – The Engineers

The Resident Engineer

3. *Thomas Longridge Gooch 1808 – 1882 (only known likeness of the engineer)*

Thomas Longridge Gooch, (3) a protégé of George Stephenson and fellow Northumbrian, was also one of that privileged group of young men the engineer trained during the 1820s. All were destined to become distinguished members of that rare breed – Victorian railway engineers, peerless folk heroes of their day.

When not quite fifteen-years-old Gooch became a bound apprentice at the Stephenson's, Forth Street, Locomotive Works in Newcastle-upon-Tyne. After two-years on the shop floor he passed on to the drawing-office, where he found his true métier in railway practice. In field work, the vital part of any projected line, he became adept at taking levels, and land measurement, in the drawing-office a highly skilled draughtsman.

Flushed with justifiable pride at the success of his work on the Liverpool & Manchester Railway, as senior draughtsman and private secretary to George Stephenson, Gooch then only twenty-two-years-old, was retained by the M&L Rly. Co. to prepare the parliamentary plans for its proposed line in 1830-1. The plans, sections, and book of reference for the entire 50 miles of railway had to be precise in every detail, with particular attention focused on the section drawings. Any mistake however minimal would be noted by opponents of the Bill and used to their advantage. To facilitate the smooth passage of a Railway Bill through various committee stages of the House nine or ten copies (in duplicate) were required of all plans and sections. A monumental task in the days before any reliable system of copying drawings had been devised. Duplication was achieved by placing a master copy of each drawing between two sheets of glass, these were let into the top of a cut out drawing table and illuminated from below by lamps giving a strong light. The required number of copies were then individually traced, a tedious time-consuming occupation. Towards the end of the 1830s the M&L Rly. Co. made use of Lithography for copying, then in its infancy. For the convenience and enlightenment of its shareholders small explanatory line-drawings were produced, attached to agenda literature they were handed out at the door before half-yearly meetings commenced.

A further impediment all railway promoters had to contend with during the 1830s was a statutory time-limit imposed by Parliament. Which required all parliamentary plans to be lodged by 30 November to ensure committal of a Railway Bill in the forthcoming session. Gooch's diary discloses just how busy he was to meet that requirement, working non-stop, in the field by day, plotting the results and drawing plans late into the night. By late November the plans for a projected line between the cities of Manchester and Leeds were complete.

What followed has remained one of the inexplicable mysteries of the M&L Rly. Gooch had decided, somewhat unexpectedly, to personally recheck the levels at the summit of the line. He arrived in Summit Village at dusk on 30 November 1830, where, aided by torchbearing attendants he proceeded to check and recheck the levels using the waters of Rochdale Canal as a datum line. The task completed, two sets of parliamentary plans, sections, and books of reference, were placed in carriages the engineer had waiting nearby on the turnpike-road. Both carriages each drawn by four horses were then dispatched posthaste one to Wakefield the other to Preston, where the plans were lodged at the respective offices of the Clerks of the Peace, just prior to midnight.

So why did Gooch panic at the very last moment? It was so uncharacteristic of the man to indulge in brinkmanship. Failure to meet that midnight deadline may have had serious repercussions on his future career as a responsible and reliable engineer.

One possible explanation concerns George Stephenson's report to M&L directors, published on 15 November 1830, part of which reads "...there will be no necessity in any part of the Line for any Tunnels, or any Inclined Planes over which Locomotive Engines cannot work with advantage". It seems more than probable that on that fateful November evening Gooch had discovered very serious discrepancies in the summit levels of the proposed line, which could only be rectified by boring a long tunnel. If that was the case, in deference to his chief Gooch said nothing, and took no action. The illfated M&L Rly. Co. Parliamentary Bills of February and June in the following year made no mention of a tunnel at Summit.

Gooch's hard work was to no avail, with the preamble for the first M&L Rly. Bill declared to be "not proven" and, the second thrown out on a guillotine motion, plans to build the first trans-Pennine railway were of necessity abandoned, temporarily.

For the remainder of that summer the young engineer was out of work until, during October he was summoned by Robert Stephenson to work on the London & Birmingham Rly. There he assisted Frank Forster, and Thomas Elliott Harrison, in surveying the line. Where he became resident engineer of a 36 mile long section near Rugby.

In 1835 Gooch was seconded to M&L Rly. Co. to revise and update the plans for its resuscitated line, that completed he resumed his work on the L&B Rly. but not for long. By mutual agreement between George and Robert Stephenson, Gooch once more travelled north to become resident engineer for the now successful M&L Rly. project.

Gooch took up residence in Manchester from where he was to superintend the building of 50¼ miles of railway through difficult country, including thirteen tunnels. In the drawing office he was now assisted by John Curphey Forsyth,

and George Robert Stephenson, eighteen-year-old nephew of G S, in the preparation of all the contract drawings.

It was normal practice to put out the work of building a new line in small units, say 2 – 3 miles in length. There being no one contractor big, or brave enough, to tackle a whole railway. Brassey, who would tender for, and with his mighty army of railway navvies, build a complete railroad anywhere in the world, was in the not too distant future. The M&L line was unique in that it was divided into two distinct parts – eastern and western, separated by the largest contract on the line, the Summit tunnel. Until it opened there could be no through-running, consequently the line was built and opened in four sections.

Manchester – Littleborough
opened 4 July 1839
Normanton – Hebden Bridge
opened 5 October 1840
Hebden Bridge – Summit Tunnel
opened 4 January 1841
Summit Tunnel completed &
Line opened throughout   1 March 1841

The 13½ mile long Manchester – Littleborough section was divided into six separate units with a combined contract value of £258,059. None of the six contractors failed to complete, although Tredwell & Gerrard struggled somewhat with their £57,000 contract to build the 2 mile long Littleborough embankment.

Measurement data from all the land surveys was made readily available to interested contractors, enabling them to price their tenders. Gooch used the same set of figures to calculate his valuation of the work, section by section, which he did with remarkable accuracy. In a few instances his calculations matched almost exactly accepted sealed tenders, the one exception being his estimate for the building of Summit tunnel, which was wildly inaccurate.

For a short period during the summer of 1837 Gooch's younger brother Daniel was employed by the M&L Rly. Co. when he assisted with preliminary land surveys for the line through the Rochdale area.

Daniel Gooch (1816 – 1889)

The engineer kept a detailed diary, first published in 1892 it has proved an invaluable source of railway memorabilia extensively quoted from. In it he records arriving in Rochdale on 25 May where he lodged at the Roebuck Inn in the town centre, along with a large party of railway colleagues. He relates how he and a fellow named Holland hired two hacks which they rode to Halifax, there they took two fresh horses and rode on to Leeds. On the return journey Gooch became sick and sore, after his 75 mile ordeal on horseback he wrote "...I was surprised to feel how little it affected me next day". The fact that he was only 20-years-old at the time may well have something to do with that! While in Rochdale the young engineer wrote to Isambard Kingdom Brunel applying for the advertised post of locomotive superintendent on the Great Western Railway. Brunel must have been impressed with his credentials, he replied to the effect that as he was coming into the north he would call in at the M&L Rly. office and see him, which he did on 9 August. The Rochdale railway office having closed at the end of July and the entire surveying staff moved to Manchester, that was where the historic meeting took place. Brunel appointed Gooch on the spot, he left to start his illustrious career with GWR on 18 August, the very day on which the first sod was cut to start building the Manchester & Leeds Railway. Daniel Gooch was destined to become one of the greatest railway mechanical engineers of all time. In 1865 he was elected chairman of the GWR, one year later by Royal Letters Patent a grateful Victoria conferred a baronetcy upon him, the first engineer to be so honoured. As Sir Daniel Gooch Bart MP, he served as member for Swindon, the railway town he helped to create.

After almost twelve years of disappointment, delay, and not a few doubts, building of the first trans-Pennine railway got under way amidst a flurry of activity. Its initial impact on the environment was both spectacular and traumatic, as towns and villages it was designed to service were ravaged in the pursuit of progress – none more so than Littleborough. There a sizeable fully inhabited section of what Waugh later described as "... a substantial healthy looking village" was torn down so that, without let or hindrance, the ironroad might pierce its heart. Mind you, once the dust had settled the benefit of having a railway station on its doorstep was soon made manifest. Unlike Rochdale, whose first railway station was, and present one is, an outpost.

The effect all this concentrated activity had on the indigenous population was to generate a predictable, but short-lived, prosperity. The lower classes responded enthusiastically to the opportunities so fortuitously thrust upon them to feather their meagre nests. Working men who were young and physically fit would have aspired to become railway navvies, older men and boys who could handle horses readily found employment, as carters and tipper truck drivers on the embankments. Many households took in lodgers, others provided meals for the navvies, shopkeepers would have noted a substantial increase in trade. But, by far and away the most profitable would have been Beer Shops and Public Houses, for the railway navvy was renowned for his intemperance.

Even the Lord of the Manor of Rochdale, James Dearden, entered into widespread clamancy to get rich quick, by lodging a claim for loss of his manorial rights. In respect of 18 acres of land affected by the building of Summit tunnel. Dearden claimed £30,000 from the railway company for loss of minerals alone, but had to settle for £150 for loss of minerals, and £50 for the loss of timber. If the churchgoing M&L directors practised genuflection on Sunday they were less contrite by Monday. Being speculative businessmen interested in the acquisition of profit they drove some very hard bargains, particularly with landowners.

4. *L&Y Rly. boundary post near Clegg Hall, Smithybridge*

For the 50¼ mile long strip of land required to build its new line the Board had received a claim of £146,448 from the combined landowners, to whom they eventually paid only £44,628 gross, eventually, being the operative word. Averaging only £892 per linear mile which, compared with the adjacent North Midlands Rly. land costs of £5,000 per linear mile, it was indeed bargain buying. The disgruntled landowners thought quite rightly they had been robbed by the M&L Rly. Co.

Leaving Manchester the line rises steadily to a point 472ft above sea level at Rochdale, from where it levels for a distance of a little over 2 miles. There on the longest level section of the entire line heated water troughs were installed during the 1920s in a cutting near Clegg Hall. The English patent for railway water troughs had been taken out in 1860 by a Mr Ramsbottom who, according to Ackworth, was on the pay roll of the L&Y Rly. in the 1890s.

For much of the distance between Rochdale and Littleborough canal and railway run parallel to each other, in several places separated by only a few yards of ground. Inevitably it proved to be a sensitive area where the contentious factions fought tooth and nail to protect their acquired rights, as evidenced by numerous still standing stone boundary posts (4). The Rochdale Canal Company, fearful for the safety of boat horses on the towing-path at these places, was awarded an injunction to the railway Bill. It required the railway company to erect a high fence or screen at points wherever railway and canal were contiguous. One can imagine a bargee cursing the iron horse as a fast moving train out-distanced him, leaving the disconsolate navigator to calm the real horse and ponder their fate.

THE EMBANKMENT

At Smithybridge level crossing the line starts its final climb to the summit of the line, an unbroken incline of 1 in 330 which attains the summit at the northern end of the aptly named Summit tunnel. To maintain this gradient through the Vale of Littleborough necessitated the building of a 2 mile long embankment which, at upwards of 440,000 cubic yards and a maximum height of 30ft was classified as "heavy earthwork". Some of the spoil used to form this linear mass was obtained from the 100ft deep cutting at the entrance to Summit tunnel, and was augmented by stone and gravel obtained by levelling two of the seven hills in Littleborough, viz Will Hill and James Hill. Travis records how tramways were

laid through the village across the turnpike-road and river, along which navvies transferred the spoil to form the viaduct abutment and embankment at Marsden Holme. Wherever possible any deficiency of spoil was supplemented by side-cutting, removal of a few feet of soil and clay from land adjacent to an embankment. In all 625,400 cubic yards of soil was obtained by this method along the line, resulting in the waterlogged state of many fields bordering onto the embankments.

The spoil was delivered in horse-drawn tipper trucks travelling along temporary rails laid on top of a completed section of embankment. In charge of each horse and truck were young lads known as "Nippers", so named because of their stock-in-trade. A rough piece of wood they always carried which, when nipped against a wheel flange as a pinch lever, controlled its speed. The entire operation was dangerous in the extreme, requiring a high degree of dexterity and presence of mind if the Nipper was to avoid being maimed for life, or killed as many were. One railway navvy never spoke a truer word when he warned a Nipper "If the truck don't get you, the horse will".

The object of the exercise was to approach the tip site at a correctly controlled speed, when the Nipper would unhitch the traces and both lad and horse would step smartly aside. The freewheeling truck rolling on to crash into a bump bar at the end of the rails, upending the tipper and shedding its load down the embankment. If the approach speed was too slow the tipper failed to cant, when the Nipper faced the full fury of a score of cursing navvies who then had to empty the truck with shovels. Excess speed usually resulted in spectacularly destructive accidents, as the tip truck overran the bump bar plunging headlong down the embankment, occasionally dragging the poor horse to an almost certain death if the Nipper failed to unhitch the traces in time. The penalty for such lack of concentration was instant dismissal, although the death of his horse was punishment enough for the more compassionate Nipper. Some became so attached to their charge they would kip down in the stable alongside the horse.

The spoil was put down in well rammed layers keeping the sides slightly higher than the centre to prevent side-slip. Built to a standard top width of 11yds the embankment sides were sloped at 1½ to 1 except at Castleton Nr. Rochdale where a predominance of sand and gravel required an inclination of 2 to 1 to achieve stability.

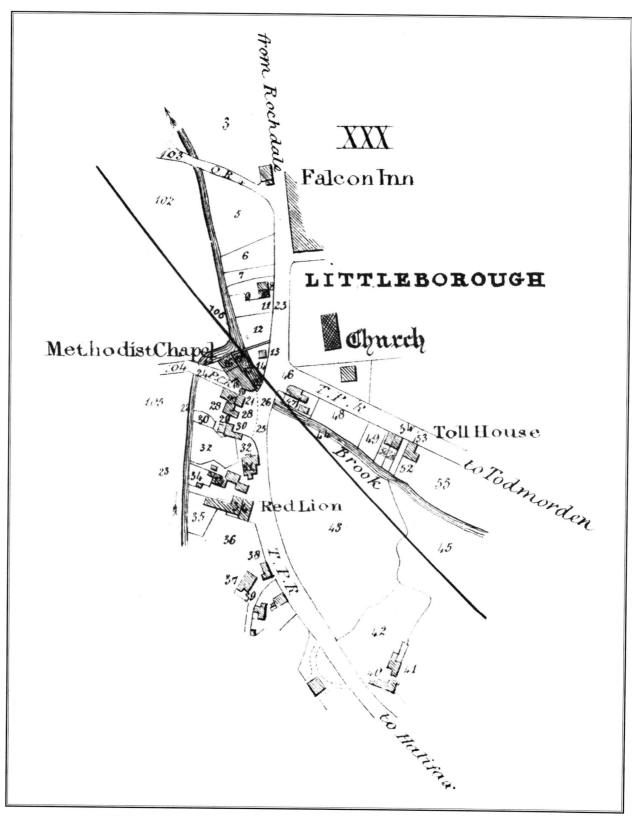

C. *Proposed rail route through the centre of*
   Littleborough in 1837

The 1837 railway map (c) shows the centre of Littleborough village just prior to building of the railway. Numbers indicated are listed in a book of reference recording; owners, lessees, and occupiers names, along with a brief description of land and buildings. The heavy diagonal line denotes the proposed rail route through the village which differs from the adopted line. The railway is shown passing on the north side of a Methodist Chapel No 16, but was actually built to the south of it. This Weslyan Chapel was the oldest Nonconformist place of worship in Littleborough, with the foot of the railway embankment perilously close to its rear it only narrowly escaped demolition. Dated 1809 and known by the unlikely name of Methodical Piazza it was linked to the village by a narrow footbridge spanning the River Roch. It remained in a state of dereliction for many years before being pulled down during the 1950s.

To achieve this line much leasehold property between the Red Lion Hotel and river was demolished to make way for the viaduct, its north-eastern abutment, and embankment. Owned in its entirety by John Helliwell Beswick Esq the site included; a blacksmiths shop, joiners shop, barn/shippon, and numerous cottages. Also included in the clearance was a large twin-gabled house of considerable antiquity called Ealees, ancestral home of the wealthy Helliwell family prior to the family seat being moved to Pike House in 1608. It must be presumed the dispossessed villagers were not rehoused by the railway company, but sought refuge with relatives or near neighbours whose cottages had escaped demolition as best they could, a common enough occurrence at that time. Severe over-crowding and consequent blighting of areas adjacent to railway embankments was a circumstance which affected many urban areas during the 1840s.

Is it not singular that 150 years on, a high pro-portion of property bordering onto railways still present a dismal aspect of dreary backyards, outside toilets and derelict warehouses? Only the cottages of railway workers appear to have been purposely sited facing a line, perhaps a good railwayman was expected to be alert and on duty at all times.

UNDERNEATH THE ARCHES

George Stephenson was the first to appreciate the profit potential of a vacant railway arch. He argued that whilst a viaduct afforded uninterrupted passage of a line through urban areas, allowing inhabitants freedom of movement at street level. Any vacant arches could and should be rented out as business premises at a profit to the railway company. In all George Stephenson built twenty-two viaducts to carry his line between Manchester and Normanton built in 214 arches, in addition, 134 bridges brought the grand total of arches built to 348. Many road bridge arches were replaced with compound girders during road widening schemes in later years.

The engineer would have been astounded to learn that his fifty-eight arch viaduct in Oldham Road, Manchester, was the forerunner of that city's 700 railway arches. They were built in the heyday of the Industrial Revolution as the Railway Barons raced each other into the booming city of Cotton-opolis from all points of the compass. Today those same arches continue the Stephenson tradition, accommodating many a Manchester car repair garage, scrap metal merchants by the score and at least one stable, home for the city's rag-and-bone-man's ponies. Built under two railway arches in the heart of the city with a seating capacity of 170 the Green Room Theatre was opened in 1983, at a cost of £275,000.

At Littleborough a six arch stone-faced viaduct carries the line over Halifax Road into what is now left of the station complex. At a clearance height of only 13ft 3in the structure is unpreten-tious by any railway standard (5). Yet, after 150 years "the arches" as they are affectionately called have become an integral part of the town fabric, and are in harmony with the surround-ings. The first official use of a railway arch at Littleborough was as the station booking-office and waiting-room, the line having opened before completion of the station buildings. A temporary wooden shed was erected under one of the arches from where passengers obtained tickets, and had their luggage weighed. Access to the station platforms was gained by a long wooden stairway built alongside the viaduct in Canal Street. George Stephenson's son Robert is accredited with introducing and perfecting a method of aligning brickwork into the arch soffit of skew-bridges to railway work, which he did on the London & Birmingham Rly. Previously the arch courses of a skew-bridge were laid parallel to its line of axis and only the masonry voussoirs cut at an oblique angle. A design whereby the arched courses were spiralled would he decided prevent lines of weakness occurring across the width of a bridge, caused in the main by the lateral thrust of heavy moving trains. The system was so successful it became standard building practice.

5. *Skewed-bridge, Littleborough viaduct*

Francis Roubiliac Condor worked under Robert Stephenson on the London & Birmingham Rly. in his book *Personal Recollections of English Engineers*, 1868, Condor describes in some detail how the work was carried out. First, a scale model was made in wood of each intricately shaped voussoir, from which a competent stonemason was able to measure the compound angles, scale up all measurements and make two sets of full-sized stone voussoirs in his own yard. When the timber centring for a skew-bridge was in situ it was covered with sheeting, then using a long flexible straightedge, lines were drawn setting out the first course of spiral brickwork. The pitch determined by the angle of intersection between rail, road, and the radius of the arch.

6. *Close-up of spiralled brickwork and stone voussoirs, Littleborough viaduct*

A particularly fine example showing how the brick courses spiral across the width of a skewed arch, like a giant thread, is to be seen under the roadway arch of Littleborough viaduct (6).

Although visually unspectacular the low arched structure still stands, an edificial memorial to the originality and genius of both Stephenson's, father and son. Although lack of space forbids a detailed account it is worthy of note – less than 5 miles to the south-east of Littleborough, March Barn Bridge on the Rochdale Canal at Castleton, Nr Rochdale, built in 1797 by William Crossley and William Jessop, was in all probability the first skew-bridge in the world to be built with spiral masonry courses in its arch soffit.

The feverish activity in the village of Littleborough during 1837-9 was not solely confined to the area where the viaduct stands. The railway company having purchased an occupation road from the trustees of the late Colonel Charles Chadwick, were busily engaged converting it into the station approach and pedestrian subway we see today.

According to Travis, the road commenced at a toll-bar opposite the Falcon Inn, and gave access to two limekilns before crossing the canal at the Ben Healey Bridge. Then forward to Hollingworth Reservoir as the Lake was then called. For a brief period after the partial opening of the line as far as Littleborough this occupation road crossed the railway at a level-crossing.

The late A W Colligan, of Littleborough, wrote of John Travis's book *Personal Notes Upon The Village of Littleborough*, as being, "... the only real story of the development of Littleborough in the nineteenth century". A truth all the more remarkable considering it was published as a slender paperback in 1890 at one shilling, it records the recollections and reminiscences of a 76-year-old resident, John Taylor. In certain passages the writer appears to have used Taylor's delightful idiomatic expressions. Of the limekiln undertaking at the station approach, he wrote "...somebody most likely knew more about somethings than they told loud up about as they often do in speculative operations". Suggesting the limekiln venture to have been something other than a well-intentioned business initiative. For shortly after operations began the entire site, and its occupation road, was purchased by the railway company. In more recent times John Travis's little masterpiece was republished in a facsimile edition (1984) by George Kelsall, book publisher, Littleborough.

The plot of land indicated No 5 on the railway map (c) is listed in the book of reference as; Land owned by Henry William Peel, occupied by James Marsden, who in 1836 used it as a market garden.

150 years on that same piece of ground forms "The Square", focal point of Littleborough township. Which is a fair indication of how the coming of the railway changed the heart of the village.

In a report dated 17 September 1838, it was stated that upwards of 4,000 railway navvies were at work along the line between Manchester and Littleborough. And that in one year they had executed no less than 1,615,000 cubic yards of earthwork by pick, shovel, and wheelbarrow. A feat which gave some credence to the contemporary belief that – The Pick, the Bible, and the Locomotive, were the source of England's greatness.

With almost two-thirds of an estimated total 2,107,360 cubic yards of required earthworks completed in a twelvemonth, the company appeared to be well on target for an intended opening of the line as far as Rochdale during May 1839. But it was not to be, a season of severe weather during the winter of 1838-9, followed by a particularly wet spring, was to delay the opening by two-months. In spite of this set-back the directors were justifiably proud of what had been achieved. And, anxious to allay fears of any further postponement hurriedly organised an experimental trip, on which invited guests were to inspect the line between Manchester and the Summit tunnel.

As a public relations exercise it proved to be somewhat less than propitious.

THE EXPERIMENTAL TRIP

Having assembled at St George's Street station in Oldham Road, Manchester, on Friday 31 May, the directors and their invited guests were seated in two second-class carriages. After much cheering and flag-waving they moved off, each carriage drawn by two horses.

Capt. Laws RN, the Superintendent of the Line, was in attendance to explain the complexities of the extensive works, and answer any questions. At Newton Heath they were asked to alight from the carriages and walk almost three-quarters of a mile along the track, past where a bridge had subsided and was being partially rebuilt. Arriving at Lane End they were obliged to wait until M&L Locomotive No 3 *Stephenson* and two carriages were brought up the line from Rochdale. Under steam the pace of the trip quickened as the train sped on through Mills Hill and Blue Pits stations. (On 1 November 1875 Blue Pits station was renamed Castleton).

The train arrived at Rochdale to take on water, and coke, but as no water cistern had been erected the locomotive stopped on a bridge over the Milnrow turnpike-road. On the roadway below a Rochdale Police hand operated fire-engine was waiting to pump water from nearby Moss Brook up to the engine.

7. *Rochdale's first railway station 1839, primitive stitched leather buffers stuffed with horsehair will be noted*

Meanwhile, the directors and their guests were busily examining the station buildings, then in course of erection. Built on land between Milnrow and Oldham roads it was according to Edwin Butterworth "... a small but commodious and neat edifice, apparently well-adapted for the accommodation of passengers (7). Fifty-years later, after numerous linear extensions built to cope with a vast increase in passenger traffic, it was inefficient, and an architectural eyesore. On the 28 April 1889, a new station was opened a quarter-mile to the west. Built at a cost of £70,000, it had two large island platforms with double track bays indented into the facing ends of both up and down platforms. Today that grand old station stands forlorn, a utilitarian shadow of its former splendour. Rochdale's first station was converted into a goods depot, the sett-paved road to which still exists. Its single storeyed station-house survived as a builders warehouse until 1954.

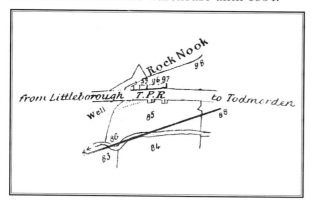

D. *River Roch obstructing the railway at Rock Nook, Summit, prior to being diverted into an aqueduct*

As the train approached Summit tunnel Capt. Laws directed the attention of the passengers to the place where it had been necessary to divert the course of the River Roch (d). Which now crossed the railway line on a cast-iron aqueduct supported by a single masonry arch at Rock Nook (8).

8. *River Roch aqueduct at Rock Nook, Summit*

An engineers report suggested a novel use for the structure;

> ... the Roch Brook (sic) which is taken over the railway near the tunnel entrance, can be used to answer the purpose of a watering-place for the engines.

> 11 March 1839 signed Geo Stephenson
> Thos L Gooch

With a maximum range of only 20 miles between "watering-places", the engineers were forever on the lookout for copious supplies of clean water, to satiate the thirsty early locomotives. Although there is no evidence to suggest that the Rock Nook "water-hole" scheme was ever adopted, the River Roch Aqueduct still stands; a functionally elegant composite of stone and iron.

The train came to a halt in the deep cutting at the entrance to the great tunnel, where the guests were invited to inspect the subterranean workings. Some of the more adventurous gentlemen were lowered down No 4 air shaft in a bucket, staying underground for almost an hour. A loud blast on *Stephenson's* steam-whistle signalled the visitors back to the deep cutting, where they were regaled with a substantial meal laid out on tables in an open third-class carriage. After distributing the leftovers amongst a group of watching, and waiting, railway navvies the return journey began, stopping occasionally to pick up stragglers who had wandered off down the line towards Littleborough.

The locomotive *Stephenson* was again replenished of coke and water at Rochdale, at Lane End the trippers once more became pedestrians for the three-quarter mile walk along the line. Resuming their journey by horse-traction until, at Thorpes Bridge any further progress was halted by a locomotive on the line. The last leg of the experimental trip from Thorpes Bridge into Manchester, was to have been completed triumphantly under steam power, but it had all gone terribly wrong.

Whilst the party had been examining the eastern end of the line at Summit. M&L Locomotive No 4 *Lancaster* had been delivered in some haste from the manufacturers Sharp, Roberts & Co. Faulkner Street, Manchester, to the point where it now stood on the line. Unfortunately while being trundled along a lane at Newton Heath, one of its wheels became stuck in a pothole. This so delayed the operation *Lancaster* was not in steam and could not proceed, nor could the tripper's train pass, as both were on the up-line. At this point most of the passengers abandoned the train and walked into Manchester along Oldham Road, the more elderly waited patiently until a good head of steam carried them forward into St George's station. There must have been some very red-faced officials on that last day in May, but notwithstanding delays and disappointments the experimental trip was declared to have been a resounding success. Everyone convinced by what they had seen and heard the first section of line would indeed open in July.

THE OPENING CEREMONY

The morning of Wednesday 3 July 1839, dawned bright and clear, it augured well for the days celebration. The directors, in their efforts to make the day a most memorable occasion had spared no expense. Too early for provincial photography the historic days proceedings are well-documented (9). The following compilation was gleaned from contemporary eyewitness accounts, and reports in several northern newspapers.

9. *Commemorative plaque at Littleborough railway station*

As the directors and their guests climbed the forty-five steps up to the platforms at St George's railway station, Manchester, they were ushered into two separate trains which would convey them to Littleborough. The first comprised of eleven carriages hauled by two engines M&L

Locomotive No 2 *Kenyon* and No 3 *Stephenson* both (Robert Stephenson & Co). The second train was hauled by M&L Locomotive No 1 *Stanley* (Robert Stephenson & Co) and No 4 *Lancaster* (Sharp, Roberts & Co). Both trains were garlanded with flags and banners, many of which carried patriotic sentiments – "Queen Victoria — God Bless Her", "Long live the Queen", "Peace And Concord", carefully avoiding any of a political bent. In an open Stanhope carriage a military band of the 86th Infantry Regiment, garrisoned in Manchester, played a variety of popular overtures, waltzes, airs and other pieces while the train was in motion. With all the ladies adorned in bright summer clothes and hats, it was described as a "gay scene", a reminder of the time when that particular adjective enjoyed an entirely different connotation.

The journey began at 12.22pm watched by tens of thousands of people along the 16½ miles of line to Summit.

Ignorant to an alarming degree of the dangers involved, hundreds trespassed onto the permanent way to get a closer look, totally oblivious of their vulnerability. Fortunately the revellers appear to have been terrified of the locomotives steam whistles, loud blasts of which sent them scampering in all directions, away from the moving trains.

At first everything went very well until just past the seventh milepost the locomotive *Kenyon* came snorting and spluttering to a halt, a faulty water pump necessitated the fire being drawn rather quickly. The breakdown had occurred on a 1 in 152 rising gradient, up which the 80hp *Stephenson* was unable to haul the train unaided. At that point a bandsman with a timely sense of humour broke into an impromptu rendition of "Oh dear what can the matter be".

To lighten the workload of the single engine everyone – excepting the ladies, stood down from the carriages. Slowly but surely the train began to move forward and would have successfully negotiated the incline had not the second train appeared on the scene. Whereupon it was decided to join the two trains together, after a delay of three-quarters of an hour the journey was resumed. At Rochdale station the disabled locomotive *Kenyon* was shunted into a siding for emergency repairs, the two trains still united proceeded to the entrance of Summit tunnel. Some of the passengers alighted and walked into the tunnel as far as the first air shaft, a few remained seated in the train. Whilst others, exhibiting a marked indifference to matters vehicular, began to walk back down the line towards Littleborough!

10. *West portal Summit tunnel – viewed from the deep cutting*

11. *Looking south from the great tunnel through the deep cutting to Summit West tunnel, River Roch aqueduct beyond*

At 3pm precisely all the passengers totalling 550 persons sat down to a cold luncheon provided by the M&L directors at the Littleborough station, the empty train meanwhile returned to Rochdale to take on coke and water. The original station building at Littleborough consisted of a covered hall extending over the tracks, its 100ft long side walls built of "massive masonry" supported a 60ft wide wooden pitched roof with skylights on its western side. Both ends of the structure which in normal circumstances would be open to allow trains to pass through, were on this occasion

closed by hanging drapes. The station platform, along which long tables had been placed acted as a dais, reserved for the directors, principal guests, and the ladies. Three other rows of tables were set at a lower level on the railway lines being occupied by the gentlemen. At one end of the station platform the military band played a variety of popular pieces during the repast. The catering which was described as "highly creditable" had been provided by Mr King of the Bush Inn, Deansgate. Manchester.

> ...all the tables were covered in great profusion, with the choicest viands, being decorated with flowers, and with various devices of the confectioner's art, small flags and banners etc. The wines – champagnes, madeira and sherry (which were furnished by Messrs Herford & Brother) – were also excellent and were supplied most liberally to the guests.

About thirty stewards, distinguished by a red ribbon at the buttonhole attended at the tables. When all the guests were seated the side drapes at one end of the station were drawn back, revealing a beautiful view of the hilly country beyond Summit tunnel.

The meal concluded to everyone's entire satisfaction, Samuel Fletcher Esq rose to propose the toast "The health of the directors of the Manchester & Leeds Railway Company", which was received and drunk with all the honours, three times three. The Chairman, James Wood, after acknowledging the compliment on behalf of his brother directors and himself, entered into a long speech. In it he castigated those despondently timorous individuals who in the past had declared the line could not, and would never be built. His speech, which was frequently interrupted by enthusiastic applause delivered with some relish. In a reference to the day when all those present would reassemble to celebrate the opening of the line throughout, the Managing Director Robert Gill said "...When they have perforated the hill which was now visible in the background, and opened the whole line, as he trusted they should be able successfully to do, in all 1840". He was of course referring to the Summit tunnel target completion date 30 November 1840, which was not achieved.

The chairman next proposed the health of our worthy engineer, George Stephenson – "His health and long life to him, long indeed might it be, too long it could not be for the public good, long life therefore to him and his". Seated at the top table on the station platform the tall grey haired figure rose to respond, speaking in his native tongue, the rough burr sounding idiom of Tyneside. The engineer began by thanking the assembly for the very handsome manner in which they had drunk his health, reminding them that his grey hair had been a different colour when he first began to build railways. In a brief reference to the amicable way he and the directors had worked together, he said that in all purposes and proposals he had never been contradicted or contravened, nor had the engineering part of the work been interfered with. In this line there had been more difficulties to contend with than on any line ever built, but what had appeared great difficulties to many engineers had not been found so by them. It was very true he said, serious difficulties had been experienced and sur-mounted, but he believed that he should be found correct when he asserted that "...this line would do more than he had ever stated of it". He continued by asking his audience to consider that because of the hard life he had had working on locomotive engines, and on railways, they would not expect from him those properly placed words which formed and graced the finished speech.

Articulate George Stephenson may not have been, shrewd he most certainly was. Aware of the fact that his captive audience on that beautiful sunny July afternoon at Littleborough were hard-headed business men and women. When he ended his short discourse by asserting "...Whoever had put £100 into this concern would, in three-years have £200 for it" he sat down amidst thunderous applause.

Speeches and toasts followed in rapid succession until at 5pm James Heald Esq one of the directors, proposed the toast – "The health of our friends who have favoured us with their company" brought the proceeding to a close. The locomotive *Kenyon* having been repaired – its injection pump was found to have been choked with mud from taking in dirty water. The two trains now travelling separately had returned from Rochdale to Littleborough station in readiness for the return trip, which began at 5.17pm arriving in Manchester at 6.20pm.

The following day the line opened to the general public when 3,100 passengers were carried. Within a matter of weeks Rochdale publicans and shopkeepers were complaining bitterly of a falling-off of their businesses. Claiming that spare money which had previously been spent in their emporiums was now finding its way to the railway booking-office, "so the working-classes could go joy-riding on the railway".

THE FIRST PASSENGER

Travelling on one of the inaugural trains, but taking no part in the celebrations was Lieutenant Watson of the Liverpool Telegraph Office. He proceeded forward from Littleborough with all his luggage by stagecoach en route to Hull. Where, under the auspices of the Chamber of Commerce he was to supervise the installation of a telegraphic communication between the town and the sea at Spurn Head, a distance of 16 miles.

SUNDAY TRAVEL

The decision by the company to operate a limited Sunday service of four trains in each direction resulted in dissension amongst the directorate. The Chairman of the Board, James Wood, along with James Heald and John Burton, directors, vigorously objected to the desecration of the Sabbath-day. An offer by the Board not to run trains during the hours of church services the dissenters also considered to be Sabbath-breaking, and forthwith tendered their resignations. At a half-yearly meeting of the M&L Rly. Co. held at Clowes Building, Hunts Bank, Manchester on the 12 March 1840, the resignations were accepted with regret. The partial opening of the line between Normanton and Hebden Bridge during 1840 also initiated a degree of religious fervour, when Methodist activists successfully campaigned against the running of Sunday trains. Five-months later when the M&L line opened throughout all protestations were ignored and a Sunday service commenced.

For fifteen-months Littleborough remained the eastern terminus on the line out of Manchester. For the convenience of its passengers the railway company contracted Messrs Lacey & Allen Road Carriers, to convey passengers forward from Littleborough station through the Summit Pass into Yorkshire by horse carriage. At first to Hebden Bridge and at a later date to Walsden, to carry out this work Lacey & Allen brought horses and carriages from their, Burnley, Colne and Huddersfield road depots.

3. ALL ABOARD – TICKETS PLEASE

LOCOMOTIVES

For the partial opening of its line between Manchester and Littleborough the M&L Rly. Co. had six locomotives, five were type 0-4-2 designed (1833) (e) and built by Robert Stephenson, and one type 0-4-0 designed and built by Edward Bury of Liverpool. According to Ahrons, Bury, built only four-wheeled locomotives which were noted for the "undoubted excellence of workmanship". Known as Coppernobs because of a distinctive hemispherical firebox, they proved to be underpowered and unstable. In 1845 Edward Bury bowed to the inevitable and started building six-wheeled locomotives.

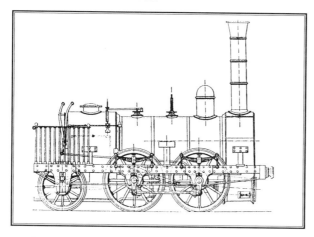

E. *Robert Stephenson type 0-4-2 locomotive*

A third class of locomotive with a wheel configuration 2-2-2 also designed by Robert Stephenson (f), which the young engineer is reputed to have said "had been put together as carefully as a pocket watch" was added to the stock during the following year.

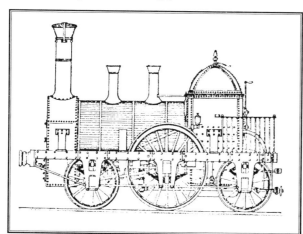

F. *Robert Stephenson type 2-2-2 locomotive*

At the opening of the eastern sector between Normanton – Hebden Bridge, and Walsden, the line was worked by North Midland Rly. Co. locomotives and carriages, until 1 March 1841 when Summit tunnel opened. Details of individual M&L Rly. Co. locomotives is restricted to the four used at the grand opening of the western sector to Littleborough on 3 July 1839.

M&L Nos	NAME/MAKER	TYPE	WEIGHT	COST
1	*Stanley* ROBERT STEPHENSON & Co	0-4-2	15ton-11cwt	£1,900
2	*Kenyon* ROBERT STEPHENSON & Co	"	"	"
3	*Stephenson* ROBERT STEPHENSON & Co	"	"	"
4	*Lancaster* SHARP, ROBERTS & Co	"	16ton-8cwt	?

The Stephenson locomotive works in Forth Street, Newcastle-upon-Tyne, which George founded in 1823, being in an area somewhat remote from where the first trunk-lines were built created delivery problems. The mode of transfer was often varied, occasionally innovative, always practical.

The famous locomotive *Rocket* completed at the works in 1829 was conveyed across country on a multi-wheeled waggon drawn by teams of draught-horses to Carlisle, then forward to Bowness-on-Solway from where she (for all locomotives are of female gender) was shipped to Liverpool in readiness for the Rainhill trials and immortality. Delivery of the three M&L locomotives each one of which was over three times heavier than *Rocket* was further complicated by a circuitous Pennine crossing. They were in all probability transported by coaster from Newcastle-upon-Tyne into the Humber Estuary to the inland port of Goole, and transhipped onto canal barges to proceed forward via; Aire & Calder Navigation, Calder & Hebble Navigation, and the Rochdale Canal. Where as requested by the company secretary they were "unshipped at Rochdale".

Delivery was over a five-week period, the first to arrive at Rochdale railway station on Friday 26 April 1839 – thirty-days after leaving the Stephenson manufactory, was M&L Locomotive No 2 *Kenyon*. So it was that the first railway engine ever to traverse the Summit Pass did so lashed to the deck of a canal barge, travelling at a leisurely rate of knots.

They must have looked a real picture dressed in the M&L livery of dark green with black bands picked out in white. Burnished copper and brass fittings glinting in the spring sunshine. Although the naming of M&L locomotives was discontinued after 1847, the nameplates of those already in service were retained. After about 1870 only passenger engines remained green, all goods engines were painted black or blue-black with no embellishment.

The four ceremonial locomotives remained part of an ever increasing rolling-stock prior to dispersal as follows; (Length of service with M&L and L&Y railway companies shown in years, in brackets)

No 1 *Stanley* (16) sold to Foxall Colliery, Swansea.

No 2 *Kenyon* (8) ended up on the London Brighton & South Coast Rly.

No 3 *Stephenson* (13) transferred to Stockton & Hartlepool Rly, was the longest to survive not being scrapped until 1879.

No 4 *Lancaster* (18) Based at Bolton to work the Blackburn line where, on 17 January 1857, after stopping at Sough railway station near Darwen, its boiler exploded killing both driver and fireman. After being repaired was sold to a contractor for £400.

The M&L became the first railway company in the world to build its own railway engines, the works at Newton Heath, Manchester, when opened were virtually in open country. But during the thirty-four years locomotives were built there the site became hemmed in by Victorian urban sprawl of the worst possible kind. Inappropriately named Angel Meadow it degenerated into an area of unimaginable squalor – slum property inhabited by thieves, prostitutes, and a large contingent of desperately poor Irish immigrants living in cellar-dwellings. With such dubious individuals on its doorstep the railway company was often at pains to curtail its neighbours nocturnal habits – stealing valuable brass fittings off locomotives left overnight in sidings alongside the workshops.

Later thieving wasn't the only problem at Newton Heath, a chronic lack of floor space in works that could not be extended, meant more and more time spent on the maintenance and repair of locomotives, and less on building new ones.

A disastrous fire in 1873 which gutted the carriage and wagon department pointed the way to much needed future development.

Although the locomotive works had escaped the flames virtually unscathed, they were said to be in a deplorable state through lack of investment. The direct result of the directors insistence on high dividends. New carriage and wagon works were built at Thorpes Bridge Junction, leaving the locomotive department to soldier on for a few more troublesome years. The last locomotive to be built at Newton Heath was a Barton-Wright 0-6-0, completed September 1881. Six-years later the works closed and an exciting new era began for the L&Y Rly. Co.

On a 650-acre parcel of land at Horwich, near Chorley, a vast new locomotive works almost 2/3 of a mile in length began to take shape in the spring of 1886. With an eventual workforce of 1,400 and an impressive array of facilities expressly provided by the company, for the enjoyment and edification of its workers. Horwich looked all set to rival Crewe, but never did. In more recent times, even this enormous workshop complex has been been closed down by BR.

CARRIAGES

The M&L Rly. Co. decided at the outset not to follow examples set by other early railway companies and name its carriages, but to identify them numerically. Third-class carriages were numbered 1 – 50, second-class 51 – 100, and first-class 101 upwards.

As to the design and construction of its rolling-stock the directors sought advice from a very well-established coach building duo in Liverpool, Thomas Clarke Worsdell 1788 – 1862, and his son Nathaniel Worsdell 1809-86. They came very highly recommended, by George Stephenson no less. Having been largely instrumental in the design and building of the first railway carriages used on the Liverpool & Manchester Rly. along with a wooden tender for the *Rocket*. Using the Worsdell's drawings and specifications orders were placed with several northern based coach-builders principally; Richard Melling & Son, Manchester, W Beattie, Liverpool, and Mather & Chantler.

Not knowing precisely what form a railway carriage should take designers and coach-builders alike with no clearly defined precept to follow, continued to build in the time-honoured practice of road transport. What materialised was passenger carriages which closely resembled the road coaches they were to supplant – bow shaped doors, roof top luggage racks, and as if to complete the mirror image, they would be staffed by uniformed attendants, known as guards not porters, carrying horns.

The M&L roof-guard sat in his roof top dickey seat facing the direction of travel attired in a crimson red tunic, drab coloured trousers, and glazed hat. Looking for all the world like an archetypal Dickensian character. He must have presented a bizarre sight as the train sped on through a Pennine blizzard. His duties were however strictly functional, with each carriage braked independently it was his task to apply or release the carriage brake at a given signal from the train driver. A vital adjunct to the prevention of runaway trains on a line with extremely long inclines, prior to the installation of a continuous braking system. According to Normington, all L&Y Rly. passenger trains were by 1860 fitted with a screw brake system (patented 1856) by Charles Fay, L&Y Rly. Co. Carriage and Wagon Superintendant 1846-77.

There was of course a psychological element in all this, what better way of enticing timorous travellers wary of rail travel, than by seating them in accustomed surroundings. On the other hand to simply transfer the accoutrements of road conveyance onto rail was an anachronism, which quickly faded away as the realities of rail travel became more readily understood, with one notable exception – The Calder Valley line appears to have had a penchant for horns, one pundit was so impressed with them he recommended their use on other lines. And, until the mid 1870s all trains leaving Victoria station, Manchester, were signalled to start by a uniformed trumpeter standing at the end of the platform, sounding a tantara.

There was a degree of experimentation by the M&L in both design and internal layout of its early four-wheeled passenger carriages. By 1839 it had a few composite units in which both first and second-class passengers could be accommodated in separate compartments. But the most unusual and impractical were the two yellow painted *Gondola* and *Tourist* carriages (g) built by Richard Melling & Son. The interiors of these curious carriages were sumptuously appointed in mahogany, crimson plush upholstery, and silk gymp, along with curtained sash-windows. The open ends which could be covered by a waterproofed hood, were intended for use as viewing platforms, enabling the

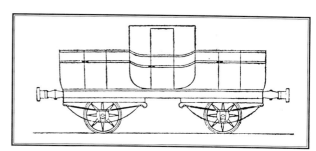

G. *M&L Rly.* Gondola *and* Tourist *railway carriages*

0privileged first-class occupants to enjoy the scenery along the line. A vista the railway promoters somewhat optimistically described as being "almost Alpine". It was notwithstanding a very scenic line, particularly down the lower-reaches of the richly wooded Vale of Calder.

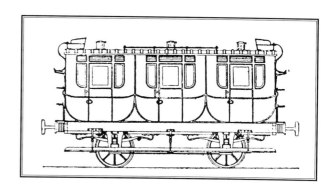

H. *M&L Rly. First-class railway carriage*

FIRST CLASS

First-class carriages (h) were described as being fitted up in the usual manner, which comprised of sash-windows, upholstered seats with back rests. Each compartment was illuminated by a single oil-lamp positioned from above by a railway guard through a hole in the roof. Conder, describes how upcast and downcast chimneys when fitted to each lamp controlled the circulation of air to the burner, preventing the light from being blown out. And how a cup shaped shield fixed underneath the lamp effectively avoided the risk of oil dripping onto the passengers, but cast a shadow. Externally the carriages were painted blue, lined in black, with the coats of arms of Manchester and Leeds on the side panels. And, as if to proclaim the lines importance which when opened throughout would form the missing link in a coast-to-coast rail network – on each end panel two shields emblazoned with the coats of arms of Liverpool and Hull.

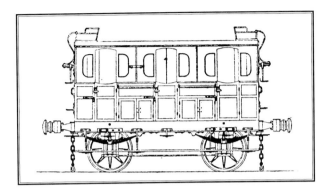

1. *M&L Rly. Second-class railway carriage*

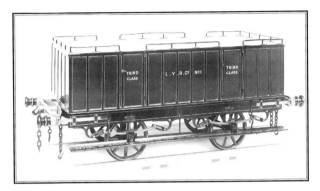

12. *Model of third-class Stanhope carriage*

SECOND CLASS

It was common knowledge that second-class travellers should not expect much consideration during rail travel, for scant attention was paid to their creature comforts. The carriages (i) painted black below the waist-line and bright yellow above it were shorter than their first-class cousins, and considered to be "inconveniently narrow" between seats, which remained upholstered until 1862. The centre portion of each compartment was unglazed and open to the weather, but could be closed off by means of sliding wooden shutters. Like first-class carriages they remained unheated until the 1870s when footwarmers were provided during winter months, but only on long-haul trains. Tins filled with acetate of soda gave off heat as the liquid changed to a crystalline state. Even the installation of rooftop oil-lamps appears to have been an afterthought in second-class carriages. In a letter to the Leeds Mercury a second-class passenger on the M&L Rly. complained that he and a female relative caught severe colds from gaps in the carriage floor which admitted currents of air to the legs of passengers. He put forward the pertinent question, "...did they serve any purpose other than to drive people into first-class carriages"?

Second-class rail travel was abolished by L&Y Rly. in 1912, but was to reappear on 3 June 1956 when it supplanted the famous, and in earlier times, infamous third-class rate of travel. In 1987 second-class rail travel was renamed – Standard Class.

THIRD CLASS

The box like carriages (12) used to convey third-class passengers were painted dark green with drab coloured interiors. They were known as Stanhopes after Revd. Fitzroy Stanhope 1787 – 1864 inventor of an open road carriage which

they closely resembled, they were devoid of seats and roofs. Divided into four standing compartments by intersecting wooden handrails, also referred to as stangs, the capacity of a Stanhope was confidently estimated at between forty and seventy. The actual number determined solely by the bulk of its occupants! When the luckless travellers had been penned in on one of three trains that catered for this class of passenger daily. Which was always ten minutes before a journey began, all four corner doors were securely latched from the outside by railway guards. In 1842 Whishaw, commenting on the propriety of accommodating the poorest class of passenger wrote "...but surely the conveyance should be provided with seats to distinguish them from the brute beast which perish". Humiliated, and treated like animals, they were even deprived the dignity of being addressed third-class passengers, the railway company classified them as "wagon passengers". At all stations a notice was prominently displayed, "The Company's servants are not allowed to porter for wagon passengers". Normington, records the Yorkshire nomenclature for the seatless carriages as being the strange sounding "Daw Green Reds". (Daw Green being a Yorkshire place-name). With a touch of wry northern humour the seatless passengers were corrupted from Stanhopers to Stan'upers, who related with some glee, how, whenever a locomotive was being driven tender first they could warm their hands on its chimney, a rare privilege denied other classes. The Stanhopers were a rowdy but good-humoured lot given to making vulgar comments about whatever took their passing fancy. Their favourite figure of fun being the besmirched roof top guard, who, whenever not enveloped in a cloud of steam and smoke would be subjected to a veritable tirade of ribald invective. The inscrutable official no doubt endeavouring to uphold the dignity of his office at all times.

This primitive mode of travel lasted for several years. In his autobiography Thomas Wood of Bingley, Yorkshire, a mechanical engineer, recalls how in 1843 he travelled by train from Hebden Bridge to Rochdale "in a carriage like a cattle truck". The first improvement came when holes were bored in the floors of Stanhopes – to let the rainwater out! Roofs and wooden bench seats followed fairly quickly, but incredibly it was 1878 before third-class carriages were attached to all trains. And, they remained unlit until 1882, and unheated until 1891.

Tradition has it that whenever respectable looking individuals were seen travelling by Stanhope the M&L Rly. Co. directors employed the services of a chimney-sweep. Who would enter the crowded carriages carrying his brushes and bag replete of soot. Which he shook vigorously to discourage the better off from travelling penny-wise. Sheep and pigs would be substituted if the sweep was away following his true calling.

It was unfortunate that passengers in this class of travel were treated so harshly for it proved to be most lucrative, with nine out of ten rail customers opting to use it. But then this was 1839, to right the wrongs of social and economic grievances the whole of Europe was in turmoil. In England the upper ruling classes fearing sedition and revolution around every corner closed ranks against what they saw as the ulterior motives of Chartism – armed insurrection of a class war. That ultra reactionary the Duke of Wellington said it all when he affirmed that he was against all railways because they would "...encourage the lower-classes to move about, and aspire to things beyond their true station in life". Segregation of the social classes on railways gave rise to a sardonic phrase, "First-class are high caste, second-class low caste, and third-class the outcasts".

It was a group of "outcasts" who had the audacity to challenge the status quo of M&L Rly. third-class rail travel.

THE HAND-LOOM WEAVERS

For generations the lifestyle of Lancashire's hand-loom weavers was the personification of an idealistic concept of free enterprise, a nigh on perfect cottage industry. Weaving when the light was good, attending to husbandry on their smallholding at other times, they were their own timekeepers, as free as the wind. But nothing is forever, by the 1840s all were in dire straits, exploited by pinch-penny middlemen and reduced

to near penury with the advent of steam-powered looms. Their problems compounded by a succession of bad harvests between 1838-42. By 1837 the going rate for hand weaving a bolt of cloth had plummeted from 2/6d to 6d in just eleven-years, half-starved they existed on a staple diet of oatmeal, cooked as porridge or baked into havercake, and a coarse bread called jannock. They also ate Dock Pudding – a noxious concoction of dock leaves, nettles, and oatmeal fried in hot bacon fat. Unwholesome fare augmented by water pottage and buttermilk, for the best vegetables, and all the butter they sold to provide the bare essentials of life. By comparison railway navvies with their threefold wages lived like lords.

The Hand-loom weavers brief skirmish with the railway bosses concerned luggage allowance in the third-class Stanhopes. Having received his quota of cotton yarn from a "putter out" the weaver would be fully occupied for a week or more producing his piece of cloth. This he formally delivered on foot wrapped in a blue linen wallet strapped over one shoulder which kept him warm in winter, leaving both arms free to carry farm produce to sell in town. The cloth he deposited at a "taker in" in Manchester — Fieldings of Todmorden operated a similar business. That of taking in grey cloth hand woven from cotton yarn produced in steam powered spinning mills, and supplied to the weaver by a "putter out", the weaver receiving money for his services only.

Although the hand-loom weavers burden had been considerably eased by rail travel. They decided to economise by appointing one of their numbers to carry three pieces of finished cloth to the "taker in" by railway. The M&L Rly. Co. reacted promptly, by disallowing this expedience on the grounds that it contravened the 40lbs luggage allowance for wagon passengers. To a man Lancashire's hand-loom weavers boycotted the railway forthwith, and reverted to delivering their cloth by Shanks's pony, which often entailed a days journey of many a foot sore mile. Whereupon the railway company had a miraculous change of heart, allowing each passenger to carry several bolts of cloth in the Stanhopes.

It would be nice to think they had been influenced by the solidarity displayed by impoverished weavers. Alas, it was more than probable they knew the hand-loom weaver to be a doomed species, destined to be redeployed as sacrificial pawns in a new dynamic textile age. Where social and economic changes would deprive them of traditional independence, and enslave men, women, and children alike, to the status of passively obedient factory hands. Who, however unwillingly adopted a new discipline working regular fixed hours, indoors, under constant supervision.

Another example of M&L persistent abuse of the working classes concerned fish. Sir Edwin Chadwick, 1800-90 the great social reformer, accused the directors of exhibiting "...the common inveterate of vulgar traders" for imposing high tariffs on the carriage of fish, thus raising its cost above the means of the lower-classes. Not until the coming of the railway did most people living inland first taste fresh seafood. Yet, when the first fish-and-chip shops opened in Lancashire during the 1870s, providing the textile worker with his staple diet, the conveyance of Fleetwood fish became big business on this line.

After operating independently for eight-years the M&L Rly. Co. became the founding member of the Lancashire & Yorkshire Rly. Co. whose total 590 miles of track served the industrial heartland of Northern England. From Liverpool to Goole, Manchester to Hellifield, and most places in between.

It was a down-to-earth no-nonsense sort of line which carried more freight than any other railway in the Kingdom. When King Cotton reigned supreme L&Y carried 200,000 tons of raw cotton annually. Sadly it deteriorated over the years to become as dour and dirty as the satanic mills it served, acquiring the sobriquet Languish & Yawn Railway. And yet,the "Lanky railway" was always regarded with great affection by countless thousands of millworkers in both counties. Who for one glorious week each year escaped the tedium of their working lives at the seaside, on a L&Y Rly. Wakes Week special — third-class, of course.

During Wakes Week mill town stations were thronged with people anxiously awaiting the arrival of an already crowded seaside excursion train, invariably hauled by an Aspinall 0-6-0. Wide-eyed children clutching buckets and spades were repeatedly urged by railway porters to "stand well back" as the iron monster steamed in. And, many a short trousered lad was soon to discover that L&Y Rly. third-class carriage seats generously stuffed with horsehair, would prickle the backs of his legs all the way to Blackpool, Southport, or Morecambe. The latter proved so popular with many West Riding Tykes it acquired the alias "Little Bradford".

In 1862, an eastern facing spur on the main line at Hall Royd Junction, near Todmorden, provided the West Riding with its own trans-Pennine route through to the Fylde Coast. Leaving the Calder Valley to climb through the Cliviger Gorge (The Copy Pit Line) to Burnley, Accrington, Blackburn, Preston, and beyond. By far and away the most favoured seaside resort was Blackpool, lines into the brash and breezy watering-place were jointly owned by London & North Western and Lancashire & Yorkshire Rlys. In those halcyon days of rail travel vast hordes of would-be holidaymakers were urged by the railway companies to send their luggage on in advance. Themselves arriving a day or so later hell-bent on having a good time, even if that meant spending a full years savings in one memorable week.

The writer's own parents used to recall a delightful story concerning an inveterate spend-all they met up with during their annual holiday at Blackpool. On the last day the spendthrift would empty his pockets of hard-earned money to buy flowers for every lady in the boarding-house. Then, with a cheery "see you all next year" headed for the railway station. The possessor of many happy memories, a suntan, his third-class rail ticket, and precious little else — a skint but gratified hedonist.

HISTORY IN THE MAKING

When Capt. John Milligen Laws RN, Super-intendant of the Line, M&L Rly. Co. journeyed north into Cumberland during the summer of 1838, he met Thomas Edmondson (j) station-master at Milton (later renamed Brampton) railway station on the Newcastle & Carlisle Rly. The consequences of that historic meeting would later reverberate around the world. He was there to examine, and evaluate, an embryonic system of issuing and checking the accounts of railway tickets Edmondson had invented, and was anxious to put to practical use. Capt Laws, being suitably impressed by what he had seen of the man and his remarkable invention, his visit proved providential. The N&C Rly. Co. directors having displayed a marked indifference towards the genius on their payroll, were not at that time disposed to adopt his ideas. Edmondson was understandably depressed at the rebuff, for in every other respect he was very highly regarded by the company. So when Capt. Laws offered him the opportunity of perfecting and pioneering the acme of all ticketing systems on the M&L Rly. at double his present salary, Edmondson accepted with alacrity, and moved his family to Manchester.

J. *Thomas Edmondson*

THOMAS EDMONDSON 1792 - 1851

Born in Lancaster to a deeply religious family of Quakers, Thomas was one of twelve children. The parents religious convictions must have been sorely tried when seven of their offsprings died in infancy. On leaving school Thomas served his time as a cabinetmakers apprentice with the renowned Lancaster firm Robert Gillow & Co. Later he became a journeyman cabinetmaker acquiring skills he was to put to good use in later life when marketing his invention. Being of an ambitious bent he went into partnership in a Carlisle cabinetmaking concern but unfortunately became bankrupt. Next he tried the grocery trade which he found not to his liking, then at the age of forty-four married with a grown-up family of his own he successfully applied for the advertised post of station-master at Milton. A scrupulously honest man Edmondson rapidly became disillusioned and also very critical of the antiquated system of bookkeeping employed on the line at that time. A system which failed to allow money deposited with a station-master for safe keeping after being collected from fare

paying passengers to be double-checked. During his two-year tenure at Milton he mulled over the problem of railway tickets, slowly but surely his inventive mind evolved the marvellous system he put into use on the M&L Rly. A system which most national and many international railway companies adopted paying 10/- (50p) per mile to use, earning over £2,000 per annum for a man once declared bankrupt. In the summer of 1841 Edmondson left the M&L Rly. to set up his own Manchester based family business. Which for over a century produced railway tickets and ticketing machinery for the railways of the world. Thomas Edmondson died at his home in Crumpsall Manchester on 22 June 1851.

Reference has been made, as to how burgeoning railway companies attempted to resolve problems they did not fully comprehend, by adopting and in some cases adapting, outmoded tenets from a moribund system of horse transport – rail travel permits were no exception.

K. *Edmondson M&L Rly. ticket 1841*

The first railway tickets were handwritten vouchers similar to those used by stagecoach operators, mere slips of paper, very easily torn or misplaced. Edmondson replaced them with a stiff cardboard ticket (k) measuring 2¼in by 1¼in, that size arrived at after much experiment-ation proved critical. Having a large enough surface area, just, on which to print all requisite information, and being small enough to fit un-obtrusively in a gentleman's waistcoat pocket, or lady's handbag. The use of pasteboard gave the ticket sufficient rigidity to operate a counter top pendulous date stamping press.

Printed on the white face of every ticket was; destination station, class of travel, cost of journey, and a small notice informing the passenger that the ticket must be shown to a company official upon request. Embossed figures printed at one end constituted the tickets progressive number, which, for the first time allowed the ticket office to check monies taken against the waybill. At the opposite end the ticket was stamped with the date and month purchased. The entire system was simple, ingenious, and extremely efficient.

There was however a major problem, illiteracy amongst the working-classes in the 1840s meant that some M&L ticket collectors could neither read or write. Edmondson overcame that difficulty with characteristic aplomb. On the reverse side of every ticket he printed lines, colours, and symbols the uneducated ticket collector was able to interpret. Each station was allocated a destination colour; Manchester – pink, Mills Hill – blue, Rochdale – green, Littleborough – yellow, Leeds – white etc etc. All tickets issued from a departure station were correspondingly colour coded. The class of travel paid for was identified by a series of printed lines, third-class tickets had both vertical and horizontal lines forming an open chequered pattern. Second-class had horizontal lines only, whilst first-class tickets had no lines whatsoever. So any attempt at forgery by adding lines to a ticket merely lowered its value. To check a passengers direction of travel Edmondson used two symbols. For journeys from whatever station eastwards towards Leeds all tickets carried the diagrammatic representation of a fleece, on journeys westwards towards Manchester, a bale of cotton.

The system worked so well that 110 attempts at fraudulent misuse were detected between Manchester and Littleborough on one day in 1839. At first all tickets were examined while the train was in motion, the ticket collector passing down the train from carriage to carriage along the outside wooden step or running board. A highly dangerous practice which according to Whishaw, resulted in a spate of serious accidents, and was soon discontinued.

In spite of its initial success the system was flawed, Edmondson had devised a method of delivering individual tickets into the hand of a booking-office clerk from what he called fuses, which were in fact wooden boxes each of which held 500 tickets. At first they were positioned underneath the ticket office counter, weights and pulleys, and later spiral springs forcing the tickets upwards. Later they were placed in tiers on the office counter, the tickets falling by gravity. At the partial opening of the line between Manchester and Littleborough only four stations were open, each of which had nine tubes issuing tickets to the other three stations, in three classes of travel. But when the line opened throughout with twenty proposed stopping-places, every station would have required a minimum of 57 tubes. Arranged in tiers a station booking-office would have resembled the pipes rising above a mighty cathedral organ console! And, with so many tickets not under lock and key, the danger of theft could not be ignored. In other words the system worked well on a small scale, enlarged it would have proved too bulky and insecure.

In his address to, The Transport Ticket Society, D G Gellard, an expert on early tickets, suggested that the system had functioned only "...in the first few months of operation". Incidentally, none of this series of tickets have survived save the odd ticket of a 550 complimentary issue used at the grand opening of the line between Manchester and Littleborough (L). At 3³/₄in x 2¹/₂in they were considerably larger than a standard Edmondson ticket, but were correctly colour-coded, black print on pink card.

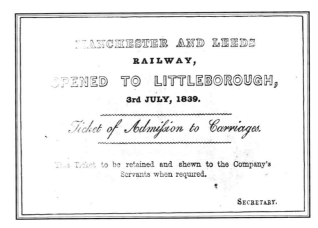

L. *Extremely rare Edmondson complimentary railway ticket used at the official opening of the line to Littleborough in 1839*

Undeterred the redoubtable Edmondson scrapped the lot and started all over again, not quite from scratch, for the face of the white tickets was again printed in black type. The backs however were transformed, a passengers destination station was now represented in graphic design; Manchester, by six parallel wavy lines, Littleborough – one broad line, Todmorden – eight thin vertical lines, Luddenden Foot – two parallel zigzag lines, Hebden Bridge – fifteen circles, Brighouse – butterflies in four horizontal rows of three, and Leeds – nine thick vertical lines etc etc. The class of travel was identified by printing the above devices in three colours; first-class yellow, second-class red, and third-class black.

Edmondson also drastically reduced the issuing tubes in size to hold only those tickets retailed during a booking-office clerk's shift. The rest were securely locked away in multi-drawered cabinets (m) also designed and built at the Edmondson's Knowsley Street, works in Manchester. It must have been somewhat disconcerting for the travelling public at large, to know that the way people interpreted the information printed on their rail tickets categorised them literate or illiterate.

N. *Edmondson's prototype wooden date stamping press of 1838*

M. *Later developments – Edmondson's patented railway ticket issuing cabinet*

These then were the first faltering steps towards the definitive railway ticketing system, Edmondson's sons and grandsons carried on the family tradition of constant evaluation and improvement of the system. What they never changed was the size of the ticket – that was inviolable, nor was the method of date-stamping the tickets ever bettered. Thomas Edmondson once disclosed how his invention of a pendulous date-stamping press (patented 1837) was inspired by the nipping action of a folding comb he always carried in his pocket. The first presses were beautifully crafted in mahogany by the master himself (n). Afterwards a Carlisle firm of clockmakers John Blaycock, (later Pratchitt Bros) made the first metal versions of the unique press under licence (o).

The ubiquitous press which bore the name "Edmondsons Patent, J Blaycock Carlisle" was to be seen at every railway station in the kingdom until the 1950s. When British Rail began to operate APTIS (All Purpose Ticket Issuing System) and PORTIS (Paytrain Ticketing). With the vital conditions of travel now printed upon payment,its advantages were far-reaching, not a single ticket need be held in stock, or placed in a

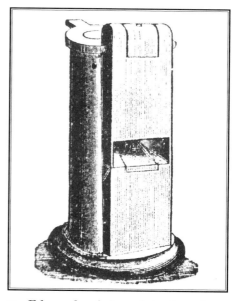

O. *Edmondson's iron date stamping press – letters patent No.8538 granted 9 December 1840*

retrieval system. And yet, this mighty leap forward also took a backwards step the new tickets are once again "mere slips of paper".

Lancaster honoured its famous son with two commemorative plaques, one marks the inventor's birthplace, the other aptly sited at the town railway station. But what better way to honour the memory of this remarkable man could there possibly be. Other than to know his peerless ticketing system lives on, at many preserved steam railway lines at home and overseas. The name Edmondson is writ large in the annals of rail travel.

4. TUNNELS

The directors must have questioned the logic of their distinguished engineer, as he prevaricated over tunnels. Having first informed the Board that none would be required he changed the tally to four, then five, then thirteen, and ended up boring twelve, with a combined total length of 3 miles. As ever there was a practical rationale to all George Stephenson's deliberations, the great number of proposed curves had come under close scrutiny. Many would be unavoidable in the tortuous Calder Valley, those at a 1/4 to 3 mile radius were considered acceptable whilst all others at 70 chains radius or less he decided should be got rid of – even if that meant tunnelling. The longer curves afforded window seat passengers magnificent and ever changing views in the scenic Vale of Calder.

Just how those realignments affected urban development along the line was demonstrated by protracted progress made at Walsden, near Todmorden, as the engineers struggled to implement their chief's new mandate. The boring of the first Winterbutt Lee tunnel 126yd would have been unavoidable prior to the spectacular diversion of the Rochdale Canal at Walsden. Work that was carried out by the M&L Rly. Co. to avoid the expense of building two railway bridges over the waterway. After the diversion the line was traced to follow the turnpike-road round an obstruction at Inchfield Bottom on a very tight curve, which explains the tunnels omission from the 1836 Variation Bill. The expensive second Winterbutt Lee tunnel 306yd as built, achieved the new directives in fine style on a descending gradient in what had been a very difficult area. It was for precisely the same reasons the second Elland tunnel 420yd came into being.

At the coming of railways different social groups reacted in predictable ways. The wealthy upper classes used all their considerable power and influence to keep the accursed ironroad well away from their estates and parklands. Often causing expensive and quite unnecessary diversions resulting in tunnelling. The local landed gentry appear to have been divided, a few slavishly following the example set by their superiors refused to co-operate with the railway promoters. Others, indeed most, with inbred Mammonish traits were only too willing to sell or lease their land.

Pressure groups reacted disapprovingly whenever the railwaymen infringed their spheres of influence. At Littleborough the church laity was deeply shocked when Sunday working was authorised to enable Tredwell & Gerrard achieve a contract closing date on the Littleborough embankment. Todmorden's approach to the brave new world of railways appears to have been downright bloody-minded. Local difficulties with antagonistic landowners delayed the building of the town railway station for years, and caused at least one variation to the approved line at Gauxholme. Where a proposed 178yd tunnel was substituted with an open cutting.

Running counter to Todmorden's negative attitude, Halifax then a thriving town of 38,000 inhabitants heavily involved in textiles, and about to be bypassed by the new railway, decided to redress that fault. A public meeting was convened in October 1836, at which it was unanimously resolved to entreat the M&L Rly. Co. to build a branch line into the town, "for the benefit of the neighbourhood". Halifax exhibiting a high degree of civic awareness, far removed from the notoriety achieved in former times. When the town meted out rough justice to all transgressors and malefactors, especially cloth thieves, who were summarily put to death by Gibbet Law on the town's guillotine. Macabre events recalled by a thieve's litany – "From Hell, Hull, and Halifax good Lord deliver us"

Halifax town's ultimate deterrent was considered to be "wondrous quick", its single-track branch line opened in July 1844, was anything but. Engineered by Gooch on a 1 in 118 eastward facing incline – it peaked at 1 in 44.5, before passing through a rocky chasm at Dryclough. To terminate in a dead end station at Shaw Syke, on the south side of the town. Which one contemporary writer described as being "a filthy dog hole of a station".

Brake vans and banking engines were the order of the day on that most impractical of branch lines. All traffic out of Manchester was obliged to reverse up the incline, often taking 20min to traverse 1¾ miles.

In 1852 the long-suffering Tykes of Halifax were justly rewarded for their enterprise and patience when John Hawksworth, (later Sir John) Gooch's successor as engineer-in-chief, laid out a double-track spur from the main line at Milner Royd Junction, near Sowerby Bridge. Crossing the River Calder on the splendid Copely Viaduct the line passed through Dryclough onto a different site in the town at Horton Street, where temporary wooden platforms were erected, three-years later a new station was built on this site. On 1 August 1854, Halifax railway station was upgraded to main line status when all passenger services were rerouted through the town via Wyke, Low Moor, Bowling tunnel 1648yd, and on into Bradford and Leeds. Abandonment of the last 8 miles of George Stephenson's Calder Valley line into Normanton to freight traffic only, had reduced the passenger route mileage between Manchester and Leeds from 61 to 49 miles.

Branch lines there would be, and plenty of them on this meandering railway. But first the minds of engineers and directors alike would be fully occupied with the vexed question of – a devil's long dozen of main line tunnels.

Chronological Inventory of M&L Main Line Tunnels

Manchester & Leeds 1st Railway Bill
committed —— 28 February 1831
Tunnels Proposed
None

Manchester & Leeds 2nd Railway Bill
committed —— 28 June 1831
thrown out —— 12 July 1831
Tunnels Proposed
None

Manchester & Leeds 3rd Railway Bill
committed —— February 1836
Act of 6 and 7 William 1V Chapter iii
Royal Assent Received 4 July 1836
Tunnels Proposed
4

Nos	Length yd	Height ft	Location
1	1705	21	Summit
2	126	21	Winterbutt Lee
3	440 approx	21	Mytholm
4	280	21	Elland

Manchester & Leeds Railway Bill
1st & 2nd Variations to Parliamentary Line
Act of William 1V Chapter XX1V
Royal Assent Received 5 May 1837
Tunnels Proposed
5

Nos	Length yd	Height ft	Location
1	2310	21	Summit
2	178	21	Gauxholme
3	220	21	nr Hebden Bridge
4	131	21	nr Luddenden Foot
5	487	21	nr Sowerby Bridge

Manchester & Leeds Railway Bill
1839 Parliamentary Approved Line
Tunnels Proposed
13

Nos	Length yd	Height ft	Location
1	55	21	Summit West
2	2885	21	Summit
3	41	?	Summit East
4	70	21	Deanroyd
5	306	21	Winterbutt Lee
6	225	21	Millwood
7	194	21	Castle Hill
8	274	21	Horsfall
9*	250	21	Charlestown
10	109	21	Weasal Hall
11	657	21	Sowerby Bridge
12	420	21	Elland
13**	128	21	Horbury

*Charlestown tunnel abandoned before completion in 1840, opened out 1846-8
** Horbury tunnel opened out 1903

If the proliferation of short tunnels was accepted as minor hiccups in a project involving a total outlay of £2,599,000, the building of Summit tunnel was most certainly not, that was quite another matter. At a final cost of £251,000 it proved to be the most expensive contract of all, fraught with problems and delays. It was a considerable sum judged by any standard, in the 1830s it was astronomical. Its current value would represent a capital outlay of £5,567,262. (Daily Telegraph Information Service Calculation)

Once the need for building a long expensive tunnel was understood and accepted by all concerned the humour of the directorate changed. Now they became even more determined in their purposes, Summit they decided was to be the lines crowning glory. In the field of human endeavour there had never before been anything quite like it, it was to be the triumph of man overcoming a stupendous rock barrier interposed by nature. Calculations showed they were in for a long hard struggle, but that served only to strengthen the resolve of the directors, now they were unanimous. If that was to be the cost of putting the first ironroad through the Pennines then so be it, from then on they were convinced it would be Kudos all the way.

But would that euphoria have been tempered by realism, had they known the frightful cost in human suffering would far exceed building costs? Probably not, for when the maiming and killing started the Board almost to a man, along with many paid officials showed little or no remorse, saying, and believing it wasn't their fault. The notion that every man was responsible for his own safety persisted, it was a generally expressed Victorian maxim that progress was achieved by money and mens' lives. The alarming Summit tunnel casualty list was accepted with unbelievable callousness as an incidental charge payable in the pursuit of progress. No wonder the directors were accused of a "... Lamentable want of delicacy, humanity, and christianity".

In all fairness it should be noted, when the Summit tunnel contract changed hands during the spring of 39 the newcomer was a brilliant tunnel engineer, with a social conscience. His progressive improvements transformed the working lives of hundreds of navvies, reforms that received wholehearted support from a new, more enlightened, and compassionate Board.

When work began to drive a subterranean artery through the Pennine foothills, the planners could not have foreseen how in future years it would intersect exactly a redrawn Red and White Rose Shire Boundary. Almost as if in celebration of the lines future role, as inaugural member of the Lancashire & Yorkshire Rly. Co.

At first the bore acquired the name "George Stephenson's Littleborough tunnel", but at some time during the three-years five-months it took to build was renamed Summit tunnel – village and tunnel aptly named after the Pennine watershed. But that wasn't the end of the matter, Thomas Nicholson, a railway contractor referred to it as the Leeds Summit tunnel. This was the direct result of many people from east of the Pennines, some famous, Charlotte Brontë was one, spuriously designating the new line Leeds & Manchester Rly. Nicholson is perhaps best remembered as the contractor who, entirely at his own expense published an exposé stating his version of events at the wantonly troublesome Woodhead tunnel.

Duplicity of the confirmed name Summit tunnel created further problems for a time when a second trans-Pennine tunnel on the Manchester, Sheffield & Lincolnshire Rly. was being excavated in 1838-45. Unnamed at first it was descriptively identified as that lines "summit level tunnel", and erroneously capitalised Summit Tunnel. Confusion finally ended when it was officially named the Woodhead tunnel, yet many contemporary writers attribute events and memorabilia to the wrong tunnel at the summit of each line. Today the first trans-Pennine rail tunnel is listed by British Rail somewhat prosaically as Overbridge No 90. Our dialect

speaking forebears were even less formal, they spoke derisively of Summit tunnel being – "a gimlet oyle".

Just how George Stephenson had intended to cross the Pennines without tunnelling is still the enigma it ever was. Perhaps he was hoping to emulate the canal engineer William Jessop, who by December 1798 had put the Rochdale Canal through the Summit Pass without having recourse to build a planned and lengthy tunnel.

William Jessop, 1745 – 1814 was by 1793 looked upon as England's greatest builder of broad waterways, he was certainly the most prolific. His illustrious career in civil engineering also included building the first phase of Bristol Docks, and work on the Pontcysyllte Aqueduct across the Vale of Llangollen, which he engineered with Thomas Telford. Recent research has revealed Jessop's involvement in the conception and design of that epic aqueduct, to have been very much understated.

Jessop had surmounted the terrain at Summit by a series of hydraulic steps, locking up an acclivity and down its declivity was a facility denied the railway builders. For them the only feasible alternative to tunnelling would have been a self-acting inclined plane, or one operated by fixed engine. Both impeded traffic flow, and were fast going out of favour as more powerful locomotives were being developed.

There was however an affinity between the two modes of transportation when it came to boring tunnels, both used the same basic method of construction alignment and excavation by air shaft. Each adapting the adit to suit its own operational requirement, most canal tunnels dispensed with air shafts upon completion of the tunnel, whereas all long railway tunnels used them extensively for ventilation as smoke vents. The most notable exception being the 1 mile long Combe Down tunnel on the Somerset & Dorset Joint Rly. which in its time was the longest unventilated rail tunnel in the land. A less obvious difference concerned levels, with every canal tunnel of necessity set perfectly level, long rail tunnels were invariably built to grade. The gradient sometimes rising gradually throughout its length, (Summit tunnel rises 28ft south to north) or if on level ground rising towards its centre then falling. Intended to ensure that during periods of adverse weather a rail tunnel would shed its own floodwater, the expedient was not entirely foolproof. On 11 November 1901 Summit tunnel was blocked during heavy flooding.

SUMMIT SURVEYED

In a speech made at Littleborough George Stephenson spoke of the amicable relations he enjoyed with the M&L Rly. directors, boasting that the engineering part of the work had not been interfered with. Brave words considering he had finally talked them into spending a quarter million on one tunnel.

13. *Line of air shafts in Summit Pass, Nos 6 & 7 in the foreground were subsequently destroyed during the fire of December 1984.*

Once the decision to tunnel had been taken the engineer-in-chief set his surveyors about the task of finding the most advantageous route through the Summit Pass, a quest that proved to be third time lucky (13). Each surveyor was assisted by a team of chainmen who carried all the field gear, Jacob's Staff, compass, plummet, link stick, sack of white painted marker pegs, and the cumbersome 66ft long measuring chains. Gunter's chains comprised of 100 links each manufactured to precisely 7.92in. Using only the basic instruments of surveying surprisingly accurate readings were recorded.

The surveyors first proposal was for a tunnel almost 1 mile in length with 4 air shafts, built on a gradient of 1 in 550 at a depth of 30ft below the nearby Rochdale Canal. To achieve such a favourable gradient would have required a long deep approach cutting at Summit, which was never a really viable premise in so narrow a valley. While maintaining an easy gradient the surveyors second attempt would have reversed that proposal, requiring a deep approach cutting to the Walsden portal, and a long tunnel. In any case it was $1/3$ mile short of the optimum length, and would have surfaced in the centre of Summit Village.

The 1837 Parliamentary Deposited Plans include details of this tunnel, it was to be 2,310yd long on a gradient of 1 in 530, with its southern portal east of the turnpike-road on land belonging to Holme House Farm. In the railway book of reference the proposed site is described as "a woody piece of ground and footpath", today it is occupied by ribbon-development of houses and shops, including Summit Post Office. From there the axis line was moved 5 chains to the west onto the line subsequently adopted. With the tunnel portals finally fixed in Quarry No 99 at Rock Nook, Summit, and its northern counterpart in Field No 55 at Lanebottom, Walsden, the tunnel gradient had stiffened to 1 in 330 and in length to almost $1^3/4$ miles.

As the boring of Summit tunnel progressed Holme House Farm was destroyed by stealth, protracted events which left the distraught farmer homeless, jobless, and a widower. At first the damage was minimal, a parcel of its rough sloping stinted pasture was lost when spoil from No 2 air shaft was tipped on it. Following the excavation of No 1 shaft on a tiny triangular croft at the bottom of Temple Lane the farms smallest piece of land. A tip site for the excavated debris was leased to the railway company by the trustees of landowner Charles Chadwick, (deceased). Spoil was then carted across the turnpike-road and dumped on Holme House farmland, at the only place where tunnel debris was disposed of on the eastern side of the village. Meanwhile the bemused farmer having survived the double onslaught soldiered on convinced the worst was over. But one year later when orders were given to sink No $1^1/2$ shaft, the farmland tip was extended by an additional 15yd strip of meadowland. Tubs of spoil were then wheeled across the turnpike-road on an elevated tramway and tipped in a huge mound, thus isolating the farm buildings from its adjoining fields. Jackson, writing with a degree of pathos describes how the wife of Joseph Crossley, tenant farmer at Holme House, took to her bed and died as the tipping commenced.

F R Condor, reiterated the belief that the canal engineers had indicated the best lines of internal communications, he wrote "the canal was the pioneer of the railway throughout England". A truth made apparent at Summit, where the railway builders benefited enormously from work carried out forty-years earlier by waterway engineers. For it cannot be just mere coincidence that the rail tunnel as built, and a proposed canal tunnel, both traced similar routes through the Pass. At 3,000yd the canal tunnel would have all but equalled the rail tunnel in length, and both are shown to have required a deep cutting at the Lancashire portal. The unadopted idea of subterranean navigation at Summit was the brainchild of the brilliant Scottish engineer John Rennie 1761 – 1821, when he prepared the Rochdale Canal Company 1793 Deviation Plans to the approved Parliamentary Line. Originally surveyed in 1766 by James Brindley, 1716 – 1772, England's first great canal engineer.

It was a measure of the Calder Valley's growing importance as a main communication channel, that so many influential people visited Summit during the latter half of the eighteenth and early nineteenth centuries. For its narrow Pass was the key to opening a vast coast-to-coast transport network comprising road, canal, and railway. Even today on the rare occasions it has been necessary to close the M62 trans-Pennine motorway the Calder Valley has remained a reliable, albeit slow, all-weather route through the Pennine hills.

Events at Summit now moved rapidly forward as preparatory work so essential in the boring of a long tunnel got underway. Carefully following prescribed and by that time well-proven maxims, the engineers set to work. With the tunnel portals fixed by railway considerations at Summit and Walsden they first delineated the tunnel axis line between these fixed points. Using theodolites a continuous sightline was projected along its entire length, and set out on the ground with marker pegs.

If the topography was hilly observation towers would be erected at points of prominence; at Summit four were required to achieve sightline continuity. Set astride the axis line and of inde-terminate height, the wooden towers would have been very rigid structures built to withstand the rigours of three Pennine winters. In the centre of each tower a solid brick pillar was raised to the height of the viewing platform floor, upon which the engineers would set up the theodolite. Access to the towers was gained by a series of tiered structures, ladders, and staging, built around but without actually touching the all important central pillars. The open sided viewing platform afforded an uninterrupted field of vision, simple pitched roofs gave the engineers some protection from the elements. The observation towers were first used to plot the precise centre line of each air shaft, after which they were not used again until an air shaft had been sunk to grade.

Everything was now ready for the project to commence, and the work put out for tender. The successful applicant was the firm Copeland & Evans whose draft contract dated 6 September 1837 was accepted. James Copeland, had some experience in tunnelling having recently completed the Watford tunnel on the London & Birmingham Rly. for Robert Stephenson. Where, it must be said the contractor hadn't exactly covered himself in glory. Both he and his then partner Thomas Harding, who was described as "little better than a labourer" were on numerous occasions criticised for negligence and gross incompetence. And when Copeland absented himself from Watford for a period of six-weeks, without proffering any satisfactory explanation of his extraordinary behaviour, he was severely reprimanded by the L&B Rly. Board of Directors, who said, "he does not appear to have the power to act when present". Copeland must therefore have been both delighted and surprised at securing so important a contract in the north of the country, after his poor showing at Watford. What the recalcitrant contractor cannot have known at the time was that for him Summit would be the road to ruin – his Waterloo.

The first task required of the contractor was to totally enclose the field of operations for public safety, wooden fencing enclosed a strip of land twenty-two yards wide. Within this area he was expected to confine his activities, store his equipment etc. Except for tramway access to the spoil banks, road access to the temporary canal wharfs in the Pass and road access to the Summit tunnel brickyard at Featherstall, Littleborough. A further directive decreed that the said contractor:

> ...shall do as little damage as maybe to the land temporarily occupied, nor shall he enter upon any of the adjoining lands which shall be at a greater distance than five-hundred yards from the site of the intended railway.

Within the confines of the narrow Pass, this somewhat loosely worded clause in the contract specification virtually gave the contractor cartéblanche to do as he pleased at Summit. Much has been written about the destruction at Summit caused during the Industrial Revolution, when quarrymen and brickmakers gauged huge holes in the hillside. And trees having survived the building of canal and turnpike-road being killed off by industrial pollution. But unquestionably, the hand of man was at its most destructive during the building of the railway. As tunnel debris was hauled up the air shafts and indiscriminately dumped down the valley side in huge yellow rock strewn spoil banks, killing vegetation and burying trees. The Summit Pass was transformed into a hideous pock-marked landscape, moonscape dereliction in miniature.

The destruction of a once idyllic defile was unforgivable, fortunately nature is self-healing, today the harsh outlines of wanton vandalism have softened. Spoil banks are now grassy hillocks discernable only by their unnatural shapes. Less fortunate was the loss of tree life, despite valiant attempts at rejuvenation over a period of many years by bands of conservationists and dendrologists, the past has not and indeed cannot ever be recreated. Sadly the arboreal splendour of two centuries past is gone forever. Since these lines were penned a more ambitious programme of tree planting has been carried out on the western slopes of the Pass.

The established procedure in tunnelling was to first sink a trial shaft, see drawing (r), which would ascertain the nature of the ground to be worked, and thereby compute an agreed contract valuation. Unfortunately the trial dig at No 11 shaft revealed none of the problems encountered towards the southern end of the tunnel. And was the prime factor in the inevitable failure of the Copeland & Evans £107,800 contract being grossly underpriced.

They had agreed to sink four 9ft diameter air shafts at a base rate of £8 0s 0d, and the remaining 10ft diameter shafts at £9 0s 0 per yard for the first 5yd; both costs rising by increments of 10/- for every 5yd sunk. That price included; excavation and removal of spoil, lining the 9ft shafts with 9in and the 10ft shafts with 14in of brickwork, and pumping groundwater from the workings up to a rate of 200 gallons per hour, the price to be adjusted if the ingress of water exceeded that amount. With the line of air shafts conveniently sited skirting the western shoulder of the Pass, from where the ground falls sharply away towards the valley floor. The engineers were able to bore side adits through the hillside into each shaft at requisite heights,

through them thousands upon thousands of gallons of groundwater flowed before cascading into the valley. By lowering the height of the outfall channels significant savings were achieved by operating reduced capacity water-pumps. At the deeper shafts these savings were maximised when a second adit was bored through the hillside into the shafts at an even lower-level.

In late January 1838, with work at the air shafts in full swing Barnard Dickinson, was appointed Resident Engineer at Summit tunnel, at a salary of £400 per annum. It was customary on railway work at that time not to appoint a "resident" until a contract had been let and work started. Whishaw, mentions another engineer at Summit tunnel, one Mr Harding. This was almost certainly Anthony Harding who had worked for George Stephenson previously, as a Section Engineer at the Edgehill tunnel on the Liverpool & Manchester Rly.

Each air shaft was first sunk to grade and timbered for safety, except where solid rock was encountered. But before they could be lined with brickwork a short length of tunnel 9yd in length was built at the bottom of the shaft. To support the enormous weight imposed on the tunnel roof at these points, the tunnel lining was increased in thickness to 2ft 6in six concentric rings of brickwork. In the past some sources suggested that up to ten rings of brickwork were laid at Summit tunnel, only six are specified on the contract drawings. Into the arched roof of the 21ft high tunnel a quarter-segmented circular cast-iron curb was bolted together and carefully bedded into the brickwork, upon it the first course of air shaft brickwork was laid. As the lining of an air shaft progressed steadily upwards the timber supports were removed, and the lining backfilled, drainage pipes were inserted at points of groundwater ingress.

At a ceremony held on 17 August 1838, at the bottom of No 10 air shaft James Wood, Chairman of the Board laid the first brick. By November with the lining completed up to ground level it was the first air shaft to be finished. The familiar ventilation turrets dotted about the hillside were not built until the tunnel below was completed. To raise and lower men and materials in the air shafts three types of winding machinery was used:

> (i) Twelve stationary steam-engines with a combined power of 212hp ranged in size from 8 – 30hp. The property of the railway company they were operated and

maintained at the expense of the contractor.

(ii) Horse-gins were used to work Nos 1 & 12 air shafts.

(iii) Several two and fourman operated windlasses, also known as Jack Rolls (p) were used to lower and raise workmen in the shafts when carrying out routine maintenance work.

P. *Two-man windlass, also known as a Jack Roll*

Too early for wire cable which first appeared *c*1841, all the winding machinery at Summit tunnel used flat rope supplied by the railway company. Two ropes were attached to the winding drum, one winding on as the other unwound, allowing spoil to be raised as bricks were lowered in one winding operation. Careful loading of the tubs to something approaching equilibrium facilitated the movement of counterbalanced loads. The varying leverage generated as the layered ropes passed clockwise and anticlockwise around the circumference of the winding drum was an early form of continuously variable gearing. Benefits gained by the use of flat rope were twofold, unlike the much older round hemp rope which, because of its twist, allowed pay loads suspended on a free hanging rope to spin and sway from side to side in the shafts. The flat rope, formed by lengths of hemp stitched together side by side without twist eliminated that problem, allowing a considerable increase in winding speed. Flat rope also layered more compactly on the winding drums, which in consequence were reduced in width.

THE HORSE GIN

Of considerable antiquity the horse-gin simply converted the pulling power of a horse into a rotative force, first used in agriculture, as a farms motive power. They were sometimes housed in substantial circular buildings with conical roofs, some of which still exist, deplete of the primitive machinery. Later on it became the standard pit-head winding gear of the eighteenth century, raising coals up mine shafts in corves (baskets). Canal builders used them extensively, but with the advent of steam power the horse-gin was in decline. Railway builders, fully aware of the economy and reliability of horse-gins were not averse to using them at points where stationary steam-engines were considered uneconomic e.g. shallow air shafts. Just how cost effective they were may be gleaned from figures published in 1836 by the engineer I K Brunel;

COST OF ONE HORSE AT A GIN

including – Hay, Oats, Straw, Stabling, Farriers Expenses, Shoeing, Harness Repairs, and one gin boy at 1s 3d Total Cost – 6s 6 7/10d (33p approx) per 10 hour day.

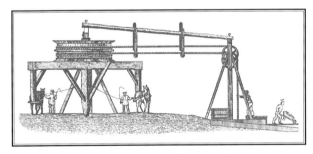

Q. *Two-horse gin with winding mechanism at an air shaft*

A two-horse gin (q) was worked by by two gin boys driving the horses around a circular gin-race. Both draught-horses were swivel harnessed to a boom which turned a large pivoted wooden drum, around which the winding ropes coiled and uncoiled as it rotated. Calculations relating to the kinetic efficiency of the horse-gin are not all that easy to come by, the engineer John Smeaton, 1724-92, estimated an effective force of 0.367 – 0.578 would be generated by one horse at a gin. Others suggest that strength/weight of rope and speed of winding formed part of the criteria in achieving a maximum pay load of 2 tons gross. To which may be added the premise, had the exertive force of the horse been applied to a longer boom, the resultant leverage on the winding drum would have increased the load capacity proportionately. The problem there was that extra long spars may not have been readily available in some areas. No doubt the gin horses reacted instinctively to any attempt at over-loading, attentive gin boys would then put the mechanism in reverse by turning the horses about and driving them anticlockwise around the gin-race, returning the overloaded tub to the bottom of the shaft.

At Summit tunnel Nos 1 & 12 air shafts both 61ft deep were worked by two-horse gins.

When the lining of an airshaft was completed the axis line was transferred underground by the company engineers, to allow tunnelling to start. A time consuming operation required to be carried out many times, always on calm clear days. The first task was to check the accuracy of an observation towers centre line, which was marked out on top of the centre pillar. A theodolite was set up with its plumb-bob motionless on this line, triangulate sightings were then taken from two widely spaced immovable bench-marks in the hillside. Once the engineers were completely satisfied with the readings the tunnel axis line was fixed, by taking foresight and backsight readings from two adjacent observation towers. Only then was the sightline projected down to the top of an air shaft, where a baulk of wood placed centrally across its lip was precisely aligned onto the axis line. The entire procedure was then repeated from the observation tower directly opposite enabling all the readings to be double-checked. Just how the M&L engineers communicated with their

assistants over distances in excess of $^1/_3$ of a mile during this important field work is uncertain. Condor, makes a passing reference to some form of semaphore on the roofs of observation towers. Perhaps coloured flags were flown to indicate the required sequential procedure.

Next, two wires set as far apart as was practical without actually touching the air shaft wall were suspended from the wooden baulk laid across the shaft. Heavy lead weights attached to the wires at the bottom of the shaft converted them into plumb-lines. When all movement had ceased and both wires remained motionless, a sightline was projected through them into the tunnel heading and marked, either by staff or lighted candle. This represented the calculated centre line of the tunnel cavity, marker pegs driven into the heading were identified as signals, which when not required were stored away at tunnel roof level for safe keeping.

As the only directional guide the miners had as they tunnelled towards each other from adjacent shafts, the signals were guarded with the utmost security. Their importance was further emphasised when it was announced by the M&L Rly. Co. that a fine of £5 (one months wages) would be imposed on anyone found tampering with them. A case in point concerned the Huddersfield tunnel 685yd on the MS&L Rly. where after a routine inspection, it was discovered that two converging headings would have missed each other by a margin of 10ft 6in. It was

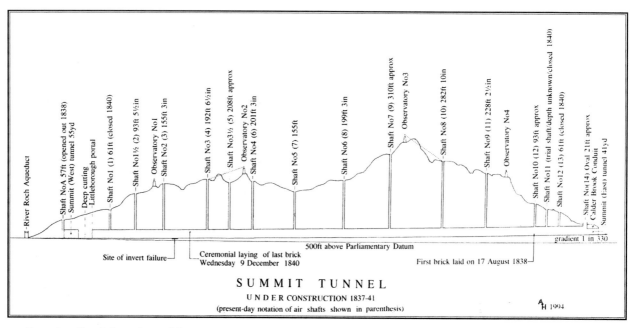

R. *Longitudinal drawing of Summit tunnel*

38

later disclosed that because miners and directors were in contention over a reduction in wages the *signals* at Nos 2 & 3 shafts had been maliciously interfered with, on three separate occasions.

The use of wire plumb-lines was at best a laborious procedure, sightings taken when the wires remained perfectly still were accurate enough. But when the wind blew air turbulence in the shafts caused pendulous movement of the plumb-lines, which had to be controlled by suspending the bottom weights in tubs of water, on some contracts the receptacles contained mercury. It was all a far cry from today's advanced technology when laser guided moles bore tunnels to a fine degree of precision. The old method was however remarkably effective, and gave an acceptable standard of accuracy. In the twenty-eight headings driven at Summit tunnel the maximum deviation from the axis line was 3in, and that on a tunnel almost 1³/₄ miles long was highly commendable. Early visitors to the tunnel noted that slabs of stone had been used to jump the brick courses back into alignment, at points where two converging headings had deviated from the tunnel grade. Apparently the 1 in 330 gradient had been far more difficult to measure, than was the axis line when working a "blind" heading.

THE DRIFTWAY

At the bottom of each shaft work now started to bore a small pilot heading along the entire length of the tunnel, exactly central on the axis line. Known as the driftway this tiny passage measuring only 4ft high and 3ft 6in wide was excavated, timbered and generally made safe by the contractor at £1 10s 0d per yard.

Designed to achieve three objectives the driftway when completed would;

    1 Establish the axis line underground before tunnelling proper started

    2 Allow groundwater to drain out of the tunnel at Summit, ending all pumping

    3 Afford easier access to all parts of the tunnel

The longest continuous section of driftway was driven by Copeland & Evans, it began at air shaft No A at Rock Nook, Summit, and extended for a distance of 816yd into the tunnel. Its excavation

had revealed beds of Bind and Blue Shale which were to bedevil the undertaking. Bind was an indurated clay so hard and compacted it had to be removed by explosive charge. The more troublesome Blue Shale,which upon prolonged exposure softened to the consistency of slaked lime, proved to be the final obstacle.

To improve the work rate in this the most difficult section of tunnel the contractor was instructed to sink an additional air shaft viz. No 1¹/₂ at the bottom of Temple Lane. At the same time air shaft No 3¹/₂ was sunk in an area where solid rock had been had been found, bringing the number of air shafts to fifteen. The Great Oval Shaft (14) at Walsden being somewhat of an afterthought it was not included in either of the tunnel contracts, and was therefore not listed. But when constructed in 1840 brought the total number of air shafts at Summit tunnel to sixteen. The first contract awarded to Copeland & Evans had commenced at air shaft No A. the second John Stephenson contract at the Summit portal, the deep approach cutting having been completed. Both had terminated at the Walsden portal, although John Stephenson was retained to build the oval shaft and Summit (East) tunnel at Walsden.

14. Great oval shaft, Lanebottom, Walsden

In common with so much other work on the line the deep cutting at Summit was yet another sequel to the grand plan. Before the coming of the railway the site formed part of a quarry complex occupied in 1837 by John Marsden, quarryman, who in pursuit of his vocation had removed some of the rock. The decision to open out the quarry into a cutting was taken after Copeland & Evans had put the driftway through the solid rock, but before tunnelling proper had commenced. According to a newspaper report this work along with the destruction of air shaft No A to form the approach cutting to Summit (West) tunnel had been completed by September 1838. No mean task for a contract of less than one years standing.

Air shafts Nos 1, 11 & 12 were sunk as working shafts, and not being required for the purpose of ventilation were filled in before the tunnel opened. In 1843 air shaft No 6 was capped to prevent overhanging rock falling into the tunnel from the Reddyshore Scout Gate escarpment, but was reopened at a later date. The twelve remaining air shafts served for over a century as ventilators belching the acrid smoke of the steam age, in more recent times expelling noxious diesel fumes. During 1973 a series of Geoffrey Woods electric fans each of 8.30hp capacity, were installed in the air shafts to provide temporary ventilation during major track relaying.

Using British Rail listing of existing air shafts they are identified as follows;

No 1 Temple Lane — No 14 Oval Shaft, Walsden.

That list includes two closed shafts, viz Nos 1 & 12 and was further reduced to ten, when shafts Nos 6 & 7 suffered irrevocable damage during the tunnel fire of December 1984.

Progress in the driftway was slow, after twelve months hard work only 1,976yd of mostly unconnected driftway had been completed. The resident engineer under considerable pressure to achieve completion by December 1840, ordered Copeland & Evans to start tunnelling. Even at that time James Copeland must have realised his aspirations and expectation of making a name for himself as a tunnelling paragon was fast slipping away. It is of interest to note that of the twenty-four headings then being worked only four had the driftway through verifying the axis line. The remainder were worked "blind" guided solely by the wire plumb-lines in the shafts. To obviate any possibility of serious misalignment, when two converging "blind" headings were within 50yd. of each other tunnelling was stopped. And the intervening ground pierced by driftway to check the accuracy of the axis line, before tunnelling was allowed to restart uniting the two headings.

THE ENGLISH SYSTEM

As its name indicates the English System of Tunnelling was especially adapted to conditions existing in many parts of the British Isles, viz. a preponderance of sandstone, shale, and heavy clays. It was only rarely used abroad, the most notable exception being America. Its peculiarity was that a full section of tunnel was excavated, timbered, and lined with brickwork or masonry before the next advance.

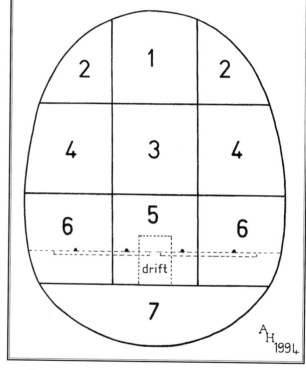

s. *Order of tunnel excavation – English system*

Excavation of the tunnel cavity followed a prescribed order (s), first a top centre heading *1* was driven along the measured length. To support the crown of the arch wooden spars known as head-trees were placed longitudinally and temporarily propped from the floor of the heading. Both parts of section *2* were then excavated simultaneously, as this work progressed the carpenters placed a series of heavy wooden sills across the width of the tunnel, on top of sections *3* & *4* from which more permanent supports took hold of the head-trees. Next a second heading was driven along section *3* from where props were positioned under the sills. As the excavation of side sections *4* progressed a second tier of transverse sills were positioned on top of sections *5* & *6* directly under the upper sills and strutted. The driftway was then enlarged to form section *5* from where the second tier of transverse sills were propped, both parts of section *6* were then excavated and timbered in like manner.

A short section of curved framework to support the brickwork was then moved into position, the support timbers being removed section by section. Once the upper arch brickwork in each prescribed length of tunnel was completed the invert or underarch section *7* was excavated and lined with brickwork, thus completing the oviform configuration of the tunnel cavity. It was entirely at the discretion of the company engineers as to whether an invert was considered to be necessary. The determining factor being ground stability in each excavated section of tunnel.

Should the contractor be instructed not to build an invert a decision would be made during the excavation, skew-backs were formed along the tunnel walls below track level, from where the upper arch was sprung. Failure to have an invert built in that part of the Summit tunnel where a seam of blue shale had been discovered proved to be an error of judgement by the resident engineer and his subordinates, for it was to delay the opening by eleven weeks. When completed just over two-thirds of the tunnel had an invert.

With the brickwork laid to course from foundation to vertex, forming a homogeneous mass of immense strength, the English system of tunnelling was considered to be the best. An opinion vindicated at Summit tunnel by the passage of time, and the disastrous fire that almost destroyed it.

Its disadvantage proved decisive, because the artisan workforce of miners/carpenters/brick-layers were obliged to work by turn and turn about between the two headings at each shaft, it was the slowest, and therefore the most expensive of all tunnelling systems.

5. ALL CHANGE AT SUMMIT

In that dark dangerous underground world that was Summit tunnel in the making, work proceeded round-the-clock in eight and ten hour shifts, illuminated only by dip candles which were bought by the ton. In so large a cavern the guttering lights stuck in lumps of wet clay must have rendered even the simplest task a hazardous undertaking.

Workmen's wages, although commensurate with the dangers involved were astronomical compared with the pittance received by the common labourer of 1837, who was considered fortunate if he earned 10/- a week. The miners were paid 4s 6d – 6s 6d per ten-hour day, bricklayers got 6s 6d a day, carpenters were paid £1 increased to £1 2s 0d per week. There were many contemporary references and defamatory inferences relating to the threefold wages paid to railway navvies.

The procedural system whereby miners and carpenters alternated with bricklayers between the two headings at each shaft, went ahead uninterrupted throughout the spring and summer of 1838. But by the autumn, to the utter dismay of the resident engineer, his calculations showed the work rate to be insufficient to meet the target date he had been set for completion. What more could he do? The workforce at each face averaged fifteen, which was about right in the confined space, and the work was proceeding twenty-four hours a day, six-days a week. The contractor was strictly forbidden on pain of a £50 fine from carrying out any work at the tunnel on the Sabbath day, "... unless the safety of the tunnel be imperilled". The religious zeal of the directors was tempered by a degree of business acumen!

Inexplicably nothing appears to have been done to resolve the impasse at the tunnel until the following February, when George Stephenson was requested to prepare a fully comprehensive report on the project. When published on 11 March at the half-yearly meeting of shareholders it came as a bolt from the blue, he wrote:

> ...the tunnel at the Summit of the country is not being proceeded with as rapidly as the contractor ought to and some change must immediately be made as regards the number of men, and general management of the work

The number of hands employed at Summit tunnel was a recurring bone of contention, with each task executed at a fixed price it was in the contractors own interest to keep his workforce at a minimum level. Whilst the thinking at Hunts Bank appears to have been quite simply – the more the merrier, for speed of construction, they argued, was related to size of workforce. Tenets that were to be translated into a clause in the second tunnel contract. It stipulated that on every alternate Monday the contractor was required to furnish a report to the resident engineer, stating exactly the number of men employed at the tunnel in the two previous weeks, along with the proposed number to be employed during the following two weeks. Failure to furnish such information would result in a £5 fine.

The actual workforce fluctuated between 800 and 1,253 men and boys, the average of 1,000 being the figure most often quoted.

After that fateful meeting of shareholders the crisis at the tunnel came rapidly to a head, and it was up to the engineer-in-chief to resolve the problem. Responsibility for the entire railway was his and his alone, right down to the last nut, bolt, brick *et al*.

Under the terms of his contract with M&L Rly. Co. George Stephenson was only required to visit the tunnel site on a specified number of days each year, unless something untoward required his immediate attention. Whenever possible his visits were contrived to coincide with the occasional board meeting he was required to attend along with Gooch at the M&L Rly. Co. head office at Hunts Bank, Manchester. His constant absence was however no great impediment for he trusted implicitly Gooch and those young fledglings he had trained so assiduously. They, he knew would carry out his terse, and often brusque instructions given *in absentia*.

GEORGE STEPHENSON
A Biographical Sketch

In 1851 J A Francis wrote: "... the Lord of locomotives was bad tempered, lacked patience, was coarse, and not liberal with his purse but with the employment of others". An affirmation many will construe as being too sweeping an indictment of so complex a character. It was of course perfectly true George Stephenson lacked patience, and at times could be overbearing, arrogant and self-centred, in short never the easiest of men to get along with. But that was by no means the whole story.

In his dogged determination to succeed where all others had thus far failed he became intolerant with those of different persuasions, and in the process developed some bizarre obsessions. A lifelong distrust of priests became almost paranoidal, as was his hatred of barristers. He never forgot or forgave those "clever men down south" who ridiculed him so. When addressing Parliament during the passage of the Liverpool & Manchester Rly. Bill one member asked the question, "Is he a foreigner"? an insulting gibe at the engineer's manner of speech – he spoke in a broad Geordie dialect. Just one incident that may go someway towards solving the mystery as to why he twice refused the honour of a knighthood, offered on the recommendation of Sir Robert Peel. Somewhat perversely he accepted the accolade conferred by Leopold I King of the Belgians.

The engineer's frugality was inbred, it stemmed from a poverty-stricken background, the second son of a family of six siblings none of whom received any schooling whatsoever owing to the family's straitened circumstances. As a gangling but immensely strong youth George first worked as a cowherd/ploughboy on Throckley Fell, earning tuppence a day, later he went barefoot to a colliery as a horse-gin driver. It was during the long haul from abject penury to the opulence achieved in middle life, first as an engine-wright and later as the "Father of Railways" that George Stephenson learned to appreciate the value of money. If he was parsimonious, it should also be noted he was an honest broker in the careful and often profitable way he handled clients capital.

That he was kindly disposed towards his workforce is undisputed, for they almost to a man displayed an effusion of loyalty towards their mentor. It was no coincidence that many, indeed most, of the first train drivers spoke an incomprehensible Northumbrian dialect, for the engineer had promoted them off the shop-floor at his locomotive works in Forth Street, Newcastle-upon-Tyne. Not that their training had been in any way esoteric, nor was it quite simply jobs for the boys, he knew they were the best. Left to the devices of the uninitiated locomotive boilers blew up with alarming regularity during the 1840s, usually when working inclines with the safety valves screwed down!

His watchword to up-and-coming engineers was for them to persevere as he himself had done. To those fortunate enough to receive his kindly patronage his maxim was "...Now go and do the best you can, and I will keep my eye upon you, and if you deserve a better situation you shall

have it". He was however quite rightly accused of nepotism, undue patronage towards his kinfolk was legion.

After spending a lifetime fighting to establish his transport revolution the Father of Railways mellowed somewhat in later life. He of whom it was said "commenced life on a coal-heap" ended it in a mansion, internationally respected and esteemed. At the completion of Summit tunnel George Stephenson was sixty-years-old and had become a very wealthy man, having amassed a fortune of £140,000. At today's valuation he would have been a millionaire twice over. He was living the life of a country gentleman with his second wife Elizabeth at Tapton House, a large red brick three-storeyed Georgian mansion standing on an elevated site amidst thirty acres of private parkland on the outskirts of Chesterfield, Derbyshire. There he indulged his lifelong interest in horticulture growing melons, vines, pineapples, and other exotic fruit in ten greenhouses, heated by a system of coal-fired hot water pipes of his own design. The barefoot cowherd of Wylam Village had come a long way.

It was not by chance that George Stephenson chose to end his days in Derbyshire. The reason, not unexpectedly was business. Excavations in the Clay Cross tunnel on his beloved North Midland Rly had revealed rich coal measures. This prompted the engineer in collaboration with two Liverpool colleagues, and the notorious George Hudson to buy up several leases in the Chesterfield and Clay Cross areas. At the time Hudson was in his ascendancy as the Railway King, having got himself installed as the lord mayor of York. His lavish lifestyle, financial wheeling and dealing in railway shares, and sumptuous banquets were the talk of Victorian England. At the height of his reign it was said that when Hudson sat down to dinner on an average day, he would be £20,000 better off than when he breakfasted. Being a canny Northumbrian George had disassociated himself from the dubious railway entrepreneur long before his empire collapsed, when, facing ruin and accused of embezzlement he was obliged to flee the country.

Exploitation of the Derbyshire mineral resources commenced almost immediately, a colliery and ironworks at Clay Cross, at Crich a lime quarry fed a battery of upwards of twenty lime-kilns built alongside the railway at Ambergate. Part of a 3 mile long tramway built by the engineer between Crich Cliff and Ambergate now serves as headquarters of the splendid National Tramways

Museum. One of the leases purchased by the consortium included the Tapton House estate through which George Stephenson put a new road from the mansion down the hill towards Chesterfield railway station. From there he was able to travel north and south, keeping a watchful eye on his many enterprises. Convenient as this arrangement was, visits to inspect work on the M&L line must have been tedious. Leaving Tapton House by horse carriage for the 1 mile drive down to Chesterfield railway station, he then travelled on the North Midland line to await a connection at Normanton for Hebden Bridge. As a mark of esteem the engineer was allowed to travel first-class without ticket, although it is recorded how he once clambered into an empty coal wagon at Chesterfield station and rode sitting astride a plank of wood. At Hebden Bridge even the "Lord of the locomotive" was obliged to leave the train and travel on by horse carriage, stopping off to inspect progress at the then unfinished Summit tunnel, before entraining at Littleborough to attend a M&L Rly. Co. board meeting at Hunts Bank, Manchester. Having travelled 95 miles by train and horse carriage plus a deal of walking within the tunnel, it seems unlikely that a return trip to Tapton House would have been contemplated the same evening.

His biographer, Samuel Smiles, relates how this untaught inarticulate genius learned to read at night school, but read very little because books wearied him, and wrote his own name for the first time at nineteen. He actually wrote very few business letters preferring to dictate often quite lengthy correspondence to his private secretaries Fredrick Swanick, and Charles Binns. Sometimes up to thirty-five letters would be taken down in one day, many of which included complex engineering detail quoted from memory.

Letters written early in his career by the engineer himself display a grievous lack of any formal education, and include some quite deplorable spelling, e.g. – riting (writing), meathat (method), a nough (enough), posithon (position), amarica (America). But, as the saying goes practice makes perfect, and George Stephenson was nought if not tenacious. In later life his orthography improved appreciably as the following previously unpublished letter shows. Addressed to Robert Gill Managing Director M&L Rly. Co. and written in a cursive hand not all that easy to read, it contains no discernible spelling mistakes. It also clearly demonstrates just how conversant the great man was with developments in the Calder Valley from the fastness of his Derbyshire retreat. A transcript of this letter RAIL 1008/114 is

reproduced verbatim by kind permission of the Director, Public Record Office, London.

Tapton House March 6.1839

My dear Sir
I have drawn up my report on the works of the Manchester & Leeds Railway as I think should appear before a general meeting. I find there are several portions of the excavations on the Line where we may expect slips – I have apprised all the Sub Engineers that this may be expected in some portions of the work. There is no other way of holding up these broken Banks except by Buttress Bridges, one of these slips I find is now taking place at Todmorden since I left. I have discussed the subject fully with Gooch as to the best mode of treating these places, but I did not think that detail should come before a general meeting – Gooch may refer to them generally at the meeting if it be thought necessary. One half of the Tunnel must I think be taken from Copeland & Evans and I think Mr Stephenson & Brassey & Harding ought to be requested to examine the Tunnel and ascertain whether they would undertake it for £40 a yard forward, if they declare such a price I think I would let it to small contractors – whoever takes it must be bound to provide as many miners as the Engineer thinks can be properly employed but they should not work more than 8 hours a day and have half an hour for luncheon without coming out of the tunnel.

I am my dear Sir
Yours Truly –   Geo Stephenson
                                       Robt Gill Esq

That letter, written just five-days before the shareholders were in receipt of his tunnel report, would suggest the engineer-in-chief had been engaged in some behind the scene manoeuvres.

Copeland & Evans, their position becoming increasingly untenable, quickly realised the hopelessness of the situation and relinquished the full contract. Forfeiting £3,000 in the process by default of a "failure to complete" clause in the tunnel contract. The partnership having experienced severe pecuniary problems went into voluntary liquidation. Whereupon James Copeland, the senior partner, got his come-uppance, as a declared bankrupt he was imprisoned for debt.

As the letter intimated John Stephenson was appointed contractor, he agreed to complete the driftway at £2.15s.0d and the tunnel at £43.10s.0d per linear yard. The contract signed on 18 March 1839 stipulated that a sum of £10,000 would be held as a security bond against his, "due and faithful performance of the contract", and further – for each and every week after 30 November 1840 the tunnel remained unfinished a penalty clause of £100 per week would be imposed until such times as, "the tunnel be ready to receive the locomotive engines".

John Stephenson

At the signing of the second tunnel contract George Stephenson must have sighed with relief for he, and he alone knew, that if any one man could sort out the work schedules at Summit tunnel and put the project back on course that man was John Stephenson (15). They were both

15. *John Stephenson 1794 – 1848, principal contractor Summit tunnel*

Tynesiders but were not kinsmen, they had been business associates during 1822-5, when, as engineer to the Stockton & Darlington Rly. Co. George had employed his namesake to build much of the permanent way for that line. Thus making John Stephenson one of the first, and in his time principal railway contractor in the land. Later their paths crossed again during the building of the North Midland Rly. George Stephenson was said to have relied to a very great extent on the contractors advice and sound judgement. A fully qualified mining engineer, he worked in the Felling coalfields south of the River Tyne, before starting his career as a railway contractor. He was credited with the implementation of efficient systems of work used in the excavation of enormous earthworks required by the first railways. Quite often employing colossal numbers of unskilled and undisciplined workmen to carry out the work by pick and shovel.

A quiet unassuming religious man who, "shrank away from thoughts or mention of publicity" John Stephenson lived at Murray House, Edinburgh, where he was engaged in business as senior partner in the firm Stephenson, McKenzie & Brassey, railway contractors. Presumably the Mr Harding referred to in George Stephenson's letter had been superseded by William McKenzie, a highly respected and reliable former canal contractor, as a partner in the firm.

With almost demonic zeal the new contractor set about his onerous task, with the change of leadership came a sense of urgency, a feverish haste, that was to create dissension amongst the workforce. John Stephenson was ably assisted by George Mould, the tunnel superintendent. Mould had a dual appointment, as superintendent and as works manager for George Stephenson to whom he was distantly related. A genial self effacing sort of man he was in effect the absentee engineer-in-chief's major-domo, his eyes and ears at the tunnel.

The two men quickly set to work giving priority to the unfinished driftway, so long as it remained segmented most of the water pumps would remain in use. To facilitate easier access in that confined space the driftway was enlarged to 6ft high by 4ft wide, six-months later it was through and groundwater flowed out of the tunnel at Summit in a temporary grip drain. All water pumps were removed, side adits sealed off – water was no longer the problem it had been.

With the tunnel axis now positively established from portal to portal through the driftway the observation towers also became redundant and were dismantled. Condor, describes in some detail the procedure adopted in the 1830s to finally fix an axis line underground once a driftway was through. At one end of a tunnel a red lamp was suspended on the axis line, a row of lighted candles was then set out through the driftway, one at or near each airshaft. With all daylight excluded from the underground gallery the row of white lights was ranged into a straight line, and sighted through onto the red light from the opposite end of the tunnel. At Summit tunnel this procedure would have been carried out between air shafts Nos 1 & 12 there being slight curves of 60 chains radius at the south end, and of 35 and 49 chains radius respectively at the north end of the tunnel. Although Condor makes no mention of it, by adjusting each light to its relevant height the inclination of a tunnel gradient could also be verified during the same operation.

Work at the two unfinished air shafts Nos 1½ & 3½ also went ahead with the same vigour around the clock, upon completion they brought the total number of faces worked from shafts up to twenty-eight. At a depth of 208ft No 3½ proved to be a particularly difficult shaft to sink, being blasted through solid rock.

Working from drawings supplied by the company engineers the new contractor also built the truly magnificent entrance to the tunnel at Summit. In the form of a Moorish arch the massive rusticated masonry is nobly chiselled, and surmounted by a deep overhanging classical double entablature. Towering crags blackened during the age of steam rise almost perpendicularly for over 100ft above the line of rails, a place where sure-footed bovines sometimes stray onto the high rocks. The deep cutting, only briefly lit by sunlight, forms an awesome setting dwarfing the impressive portal which can be viewed from a vantage point on the road above.

Bricks & Mortar

If beds of clay in sufficient quantity and of the right quality were revealed in the excavations of a long rail tunnel, it made economic sense to have the tunnel lining brick manufactured on site. A temporary claymill and kilns would be set up to produce a product which often achieved savings of 10/- per 1,000 brick against 1830s retail prices. Should coal measures also be discovered in the workings, that too would be used to advantage in firing the kilns, a further bonus.

By a geological caprice no satisfactory clay emerged from the Summit tunnel excavations. Ironically on a hillside opposite, almost within hailing distance, the Pass positively abounded with a high quality loam which promoted and sustained large-scale sanitary ware and brickmaking enterprises for well over a century, eating away half a hillside in the process. Travis, lists three local brickfields in chronological order; 1 Punchbowl at Summit, 2 Rake, Littleborough, 3 Chelburn, Summit, but is vague about precise dates. At one point he appears to imply that all had operated during the post railway era, but then confuses the issue by asserting that patent machinery at the giant Chelburn Plant was initially powered by water turbine, which would suggest an earlier period. It is of course well-documented that the Punchbowl works commenced operations during the post canal era. What is also known is the proven fact that none of the above were in anyway involved with the subject matter of this chapter. The brick used to line Summit tunnel, costing £46,000 was transported 16½ miles by rail and road haulage from Manchester to the top of the air shafts – all 23 million of them.

In 1837 William Higgins, was trading as a master brickmaker at Cheetham Hill Road, Manchester, his brickfield on an elevated site within 400yd of the railway was ideally situated to supply the many millions of brick required to build the new line. A self-acting tramway built on wooden trestles transferred the brick from kiln to railway. Loaded wagons pulling empty ones back up the incline by rope haulage. At this juncture it is perhaps worth a passing glance at the time consuming occupation of brickmaking during the pre-mechanised period of the early nineteenth century.

The handmade bricks were individually formed in open wooden moulds by the cheap and plentiful labour of women and children, who were paid a mere pittance. Puddled clay was rammed into the wooden moulds, surplus clay being removed by the deft stroke of a stick passed across the top lip of the mould. Nimble fingers then eased the mould upwards to reveal one unfrogged brick, correctly spaced in serried ranks the raw bricks were then wheeled into the kilns for firing.

Work in a brickfield was carried out on open ground under open sided shades which gave minimal protection against the elements. In appalling conditions of wet and intense cold, some children stood barefoot until they had earned enough money to buy a pair of wooden-soled clogs.

A days work was regulated by daylight hours, many toiled quite literally from dawn to dusk, a fourteen, even sixteen-hour day being commonplace. Totally exhausted the "brickfield maidens", as the women were called, and their wretched offspring shuffled homeward after a hard days work, to insalubrious back-street hovels and squalid courtyards, their ragged clothing and skin caked in dried clay. To the railway promoters their efforts represented real progress, for the brickfield maidens driven by poverty it was more mundane, a question of sustenance for their hungry brood.

The specification for the Summit tunnel bricks required that all should be, "well-shapen and evenly burned". The contractor, on pain of yet another fine was forbidden to use any deformed or cracked bricks in the tunnel lining. But was allowed to dispose of faulty brick, and brick-bats when forming a well-compacted infill behind the tunnel lining.

William Higgins brick was first used by the M&L Rly. Co. to build the half-mile long fifty-eight arch viaduct in Oldham Road, Manchester. The original terminus of the line had its platforms on this viaduct, its ticket office/waiting room sited at street level underneath it. The elevated line was the unavoidable result of George Stephenson's unequivocal insistence on easy gradients, consequently Manchester's second railway station was an elevated dead-end terminus that proved inconvenient to operate. Designed by the engineer two enormous platform hoists capable of handling 1,000 tons daily transferred goods between the upper and lower-levels, both were later replaced with an inclined plane.

When, after much protracted wrangling between the L&M Rly. Co. and M&L Rly. Co. a coast-to-coast railway network between the cities of Liverpool and Hull had been achieved – by extending the M&L from Miles Platting for a distance of 2 mile 572yd to join an extended L&M line at the new Victoria station (Hunts Bank) in 1844, St George's station was bypassed. After operating as the lines principal main line passenger station for rather less than five-years, St George's was unceremoniously converted into an eight acre goods depot. Its fate was sealed just two days before the station opened its doors to fare paying passengers, when the Royal Assent was given to the M&L Rly. Co. Act authorising an extension of the line into Hunts Bank on 1 July 1839.

Earlier it had been a very different story as the nerve centre and main supply base much attention had been focused on the station. In 1839 a newspaper reporter noted that alongside the viaduct, close by the station, a sawmill was to be seen producing wooden railway sleepers by the thousand. Nearby he saw a horse-gin turning a mortar mill, workmen were everywhere, and adding to the hurried activity was the delivery of brick down the aerial tramway onto the viaduct for loading into the Littleborough brick trains. Which, coupled with the arrival and departure of passenger trains, served only to highlight the frenetic clamour and former importance of St George's station.

The Summit tunnel bricks were transported by rail free of any charge, the contractor providing all necessary labour, ancillary equipment, building temporary roads, and staging entirely at his own expense.

In all probability the skeletal passenger service operating between Manchester and Littleborough after partial opening in July 1839, functioned on a push-pull system, using the up-line, leaving the down-line clear for brick trains. With every brick handled individually a fully laden brick train would have blocked the main line for an inordinate length of time during unloading. This hypothesis is strengthened on two counts; at a standard top width of 11yd the Littleborough embankment would not have been wide enough to accommodate a single-track siding. Also, no sidings temporary or otherwise are indicated on the 6in Ordnance Survey Map, *Lancashire* (first edition sheet 81). However in the same area where the Summit tunnel bricks were off-loaded triple tracked sidings were built at a later date by widening the 30ft high embankment for a distance of 733yd.

Wooden chutes laid down the embankment were used to transfer brick to field level at Featherstall, Littleborough, where a parcel of land had been leased by the railway company for the duration of the tunnel contract. There under the watchful eye of one Mr Allcock, manager, they were sorted into grades, stacked, and no doubt counted prior to being taken by road to the air shafts. An 1840 newspaper sales advertisement indicated that the Summit Tunnel Brickyard, at Featherstall, was very conveniently sited close to railway, canal, and turnpike road. Which would suggest the Stubley Mill Road – Box Street area, the brickyard predating all existing property.

Temporary wooden bridges were hastily thrown across the River Roch which flows through the flat fields at Featherstall, and the entire brickyard area securely fenced to provide safe grazing for the many horses used. Within this area temporary wooden buildings offered makeshift accommodation for the many labourers, carters, resident farriers, stabling, harness rooms, and dry storage of forage – hay, oats, and bedding straw. In addition, some open sided wooden structures known as shades provided a degree of protection, for one of Mr Allcock's most important duties was to ensure the bricks retained an acceptable level of moisture content. Too dry they would be doused with water, too wet the brick-layers were unable to lay them.

The sheer size of this hitherto historically neglected part of the great undertaking may be gauged from figures published in the February 1840 issue of the *Civil Engineers & Architects Journal*. At maximum output the tunnel brick-layers were laying 51,000 – 60,000 bricks a day, figures that represented the absolute minimum number of brick required to be carted daily from brickyard to tunnel to maintain output. But, because the movement of brick was used to calculate two interim payments – money the con-tractor needed to settle his not inconsiderable bi-weekly wages bill, John Stephenson moved the brick in prodigious quantities, using "54 draught-horses"(sic) and an undisclosed number of carts and waggons in the process. This is most probably a printers error and should read, "154 draught-horses", as two other mostly reliable sources list the number of horses used by John Stephenson at 130 and 150 respectively. When-ever the contractor had 2 million bricks on site, but unused, he received a subsistence allowance equal to half their kiln value. Whishaw valued the brick at £2 per 1,000 delivered at the shafts. This figure included the George III brick tax, originally levied at 2/6d per 1,000 but which rose to 6/6d during the railway era and was repealed in 1850. A further monthly progress payment of £2 for every yard of completed tunnel lining was also made.

Weighing something approaching 100,000 tons in total the bricks were carted from the brickyard over steadily rising ground, through Calderbrook village for a distance of 3 miles into very difficult country at the air shafts. In 1855, the writer Edwin Waugh commented that the thoroughfare between Featherstall and Calderbrook was "... a rough old road". It was, and still is quite steep in parts, where teams of chain horses waited to haul brick carts up the more difficult gradients. Places where carters cursed, whips cracked, and sweating horses strained, the entire enterprise now forgotten was an outstanding achievement by both horse and man.

Somewhere along the line someone got their sums wrong, leaving almost half a million brick on the ground at Featherstall surplus to requirements. They were offered for sale on Wednesday 6 May 1840 by Richard Sellars, auctioneer of Rochdale, along with other tunnel artefacts. Included in the sale were, 440,000 bricks plus a quantity of fire brick, wooden sheds, shades and fire-holes, drainage tiles, gearing, and fourteen of the draught-horses, which the auctioneer respectfully wished to bring to the especial attention of farmers.

The brick must not have been very durable or was damaged by the chemical content of groundwater, which percolated through the tunnel lining. In common with most early Victorian railway tunnels the Summit has over the years been totally relined.

As the bricks arrived at Summit from the west the cement on which they were to be bedded was in transit from the east. 8,000 tons of Roman Cement purchased from near Hull at 2/6d per bushel, was transhipped onto canal barges, for passage along the Aire & Calder Navigation, Calder & Hebble Navigation, and Rochdale Canal, to be off-loaded at various points within the Summit Pass. The work of building and eventual removal of these temporary wharfs was carried out by John Stephenson.

Roman Cement was so named because it was purported to make mortar as hard and durable as the best specimens surviving from the Roman occupation of Britain. It was manufactured by grinding and burning the soft brown calcareous nodules found in the London clay at Harwich and Sheppey. At the time it was a relatively new product having been patented as recently as 1796, on site it was mixed with equal parts of clean sharp sand to form a bedding matrix. The rapid hardening cement was chosen for use at Summit solely because of its impermeability to water. A quality that was initially sustained, for several early visitors to the tunnel commented on the dry state of the tunnel lining. Today the tunnel may be said to be, not quite so dry.

By December 1839 John Stephenson was a supremely happy man, his sound judgement and organisational skills had by then, increased the rate of progress in the tunnel from 85yd during the first month of his contract, to well over 200yd that December. The following April he planned to have all the brick on site, neatly stacked at the tops of the air shafts, in consequence of which he would be in receipt of a substantial advance payment. He was also very confident that the completion date of 30 November 1840 could and would be met. With things going so well. and in keeping with the festive season, the contractor decided to show his gratitude to the entire team of tunnel inspectors for their efficient overseeing of the great work.

THE DINNER PARTY

At the Falcon Inn, Littleborough, on Thursday 16 January 1840, seventy of John Stephenson's honoured guests sat down to a substantial dinner provided by the landlord Isaac Marsden. A band of music opened the proceedings with the national anthem, and continued to entertain the guests during the repast. On the cloth being drawn a party of glee singers gave *Non Nobis Domine* (*Not unto us o Lord*, Psalm CXV) a customary oblation offered at all special occasions, this being followed by the usual loyal toasts.

Afterwards the evening settled down to a series of toasts and speeches interspersed with music. From the chair John Stephenson gave the toast, The health of George Stephenson, the "Father of railways", which was greeted by loud and prolonged cheering. The great engineer notable only on this auspicious occasion by his continued absence. As the night wore on toast followed toast in a very precise pecking order. George Mould, the indefatigable superintendent at the tunnel gave the toast, "The Summit tunnel" which he followed with a long speech replete of professional information detailing progress at the tunnel. Unfortunately because an editor decided the speech was too technical and overlong for inclusion in a newspaper report of the dinner, valuable first-hand knowledge relating to the tunnel was irrevocably lost. The toast "The whole of the inspectors on the Summit tunnel" was acknowledged by Inspector Taylor. It is of interest to note that Dr. Barker, surgeon to the Summit Tunnel Sickness & Burial Benefit Society also attended the dinner. The STS&BBS will be examined at length in a subsequent chapter.

After listing fifteen toasts the *Manchester Guardian* newspaper report concluded with, "and many other toasts followed, and the company broke up when morning again called them forth to the works". No doubt with many a sore head.

16. *Silver banqueting table centrepiece in the form of a model of Summit tunnel, with figurines of Thomas L Gooch (left) and George Stephenson*

John Stephenson's euphoria was to be short-lived; discontent amongst his workforce was widespread, resulting in the bricklayers forming themselves into a combination. It was all perfectly legal of course, the Combination Acts of 1799 banning the formation of trade unions had been repealed 1824-5. For workers desperately trying to improve their lot it was an uphill struggle; most employers simply ignored the law and would have nothing whatsoever to do with organised labour. The management at Summit tunnel talked glibly of the advantages resulting from a reciprocity of feeling between master and men. But these were early days of organised trades unionism and with both sides deeply entrenched confrontation was inevitable.

Perhaps John Stephenson honestly thought the threefold wages he paid debarred the men from all complaint – his brickies thought otherwise. Indeed, what happened next – it came to be known as the "Turnout of Bricklayers at Summit" – would undoubtedly have ended as a nine-days wonder had it not been for an extraordinary act on the part of the contractor. During March 1840 with all work at the tunnel stopped John Stephenson tried to break the strike by hiring thirty-two bricklayers from the recently completed South Shields tunnel, offering them six-months work at 5/- a day. But why six-months? Was he planning to finish the tunnel three-months ahead of schedule, and using cheap labour to boot. At any rate the old hands would have none of it, on the morning of Saturday 21 March they decoyed the newcomers with a promissory payment of 35/- for each man if he would agree to return home, and spirited them away from the tunnel.

Retribution was swift, the sixteen ringleaders of the bricklayers' combination were arrested. On the following Tuesday at the Rochdale Police Office, they were arraigned before Clement Royds and W Chadwick, magistrates, charged with intimidation and preventing other workmen from following their lawful employment. Mr Hunt, a solicitor, informed the bench that his client John Stephenson had learned that the affair was affected by a conspiracy of such bricklayers as were in a trade union, and that most of the offenders had been seen entering the club house in Manchester. The accused were brought up before the magistrates four at a time to make their defence statements, which it was reported varied much. Six or seven were committed to three-months hard labour, a few to one month, the others were permitted to return to the tunnel on promises of amendment. The contractor then tried a different tack. In May, after a few weeks of uneasy peace at the tunnel, he offered the bricklayers an extra days pay for every foot of progress beyond an agreed measure – a financial inducement the wily brickies found to be most

acceptable. Between June and October £1,075 was paid out in incentive bonuses. The system was deemed to have been so successful by all concerned it was adopted at Bramhope tunnel, on the Leeds & Thirsk Rly.

The Summit tunnel bricklayers struggle was in many ways understandable for this was a period of tumultuous change. To right the wrongs of grievous social injustices the rallying cry of the toiling masses during the thirties and hungry forties was Chartism. The movement was in its ascendancy following the temporary demise of trades unionism. Members paid one penny subscription and wore red caps to proclaim their allegiance, but in the end the movement failed. A revival of trades unionism and co-operative movements then took up the cudgel for emancipation of the labouring masses – they in turn fathered the Labour Party.

The first Reform Bill of 1832 had done next to nothing to alleviate the suffering of the lower-classes, the harsh treatment of the destitute in workhouses hung over them like the sword of Damocles. Inevitably there were many desperate, and extremely dangerous men at large.

But really, who were those boisterous yet colourful characters who arrived at Summit as if from nowhere, stayed for three-years, then just as suddenly vanished. Leaving the tiny village to reflect on what had happened, and clear up the appalling mess? They were in fact the proverbial Englishman, Irishman and Scotsman, rip-roaring malcontents hell-bent on trans-forming the beautiful Summit Pass into a premature Klondike, not by prospecting but to go a-navvying.

6. NAVVIES AND SHANTIES

It used to be said that a prerequisite for the making of a good railway navvy was, prodigious physical strength plus the ability to consume two pounds of beef, two pounds of bread, and a gallon of beer daily. An affirmation which underlined the fact that the work was extremely hard and the lifestyle rough. The collective name used to characterise the builders of railways – "railway navvies" is in someways a misnomer. Many contemporary writers, magistrates, even contractors, referred to the workers as excavators/labourers, or by the trade they followed, only rarely as navvies. And, as if to further confuse matters the name Tunnel Tigers has been bandied about of late as the name adopted by railway tunnel face workers. A pseudonym conjuring up the image of proud bravadoes displaying their superior prowess, alas, there is little or no evidence to corroborate the claim that such a jingoistic name was ever widely adopted, except that is in works of fiction. Always a man of forthright demeanour who never minced his words, George Stephenson spoke of his men at Summit tunnel as being mineworkers. Be that as it may, all without exception, are now instantly recognised as history has recorded them, by the generic name – The Railway Navvies.

Lured by tales of unheard of affluence they came in tens of thousands to work on the ironroad – farmhands, quarrymen, fenmen, and coalminers. Older men whose working lives had spanned the transition from canal to rail travel were often employed as overlookers or gangers, others were the sons of navigators. All had an innate knowledge of earthwork and understood the nature of clay and rock, organic substances the navvy always referred to as "muck". Although dissolute and totally uneducated except that is in worldly attributes, the railway navvy was all things to all men; To a contractor he represented an uncomplaining and willing worker, to publicans, shopkeepers, and landlords a highly profitable if transitory boost to trade, as an habitual poacher he was the sworn enemy of all farmers, gamekeepers and landowners. By the populace at large he was both feared and admired.

His exceptionally high earnings, uncouth habits, belligerent behaviour especially when in drink, bad language, and ostentatious clothing, alienated the navvy from almost all social groups. The description given by Samuel Smiles, in his *Lives of the Engineers*, of a railway navvy's wearing apparel reads like the sartorial elegance of a rustic. "A white felt hat with upturned brim, a velveteen or jean square tailed coat, scarlet plush waistcoat with little black spots, a brightly coloured kerchief loosely tied around the neck, corduroy breeches tied at the knee, and strong high-laced boots." Smiles, was of course referring to navvies working in the south of the country, and on the London & Birmingham Rly. in particular. Fashions can and do have regional variants, navvies at work on the M&L Rly. would appear to have been clad similar to those depicted in (p). Double canvas open necked shirts, moleskin (double twilled fustian) breeches tied at the knee, and high-laced hobnailed boots being standard navvy wear.

The importance attached to footwear – known in navvy slang as his "Bluchers" (after the Prussian Field Marshal) and more descriptively as his "understandins" – was such that should a navvy's boots be in poor condition a contractor would not employ him. A tale was told of one railway navvy having secured very comfortable lodgings with a comely widow, who fed and bedded him; she even provided him with tobacco. He repaid such kindness by decamping without paying his dues, wearing her son's boots! In the context of work apparel it is perhaps noteworthy to record that during the 1850s and possibly earlier, male operatives in the Lancashire textile industry also wore white felt hats. Where they became known as "bobbin nudgers" and "wideawakes".

At the boring of any long railway tunnel the workforce formed four distinct categories of personnel, each one of which could be subdivided into named groups of artisans, ancillary operatives and officials; 1. Men at work performing the initial task, that of sinking air shafts were known collectively, and not entirely unexpectedly as Sinkers. Included were excavators, winders, general labourers, carpenters, and bricklayers /stonemasons: 2. Once the revetting of a shaft was completed it was worked as a supply artery, and lifeline for the underground workers immediately below, by teams of top and bottom men. Those on the surface comprised winders, bucket-steerers and labourers handling tubs of brick or wheeling tubs of clay and rock along tramways to the spoil banks. All these men worked under the supervision of a Banksman. In charge of stationary steam engines, boilers, and winding machinery were the blue overalled mechanics, firemen, oilers and greasers and engine-tenters. All were known somewhat conversely as the Black Gang – reputedly the hardest drinkers. At the shaft bottom labourers wheeled tubs of spoil into position in readiness for hoisting and pushed loaded tubs of brick forward into the heading.

Below the wooden platform on which they stood other workmen down in the shaft sump checked the water level, ensured the side drainage grips flowed freely and regularly cleaned the water pump filters. All these men were at high risk from falling objects: 3. In every tunnel heading a team of hand-picked and highly paid men formed the elite corps of the entire tunnel workers – drillers /shakers/jumpers, shot-firers, getters, labourers, carpenters, and bricklayers. In charge of the excavators/miners was a Ganger experienced in the use of explosives: 4. The supervisory staff listed in order of authority were, the resident tunnel engineer and his subordinates, the engineer-in-chiefs manager, tunnel superintendent, tunnel inspectorate, contractor's agents, subcontractor's representatives, overlookers and gangers.

The more enterprising navvies formed themselves into gangs of ten, twelve, even twenty men called Butty Gangs, who opted to execute set amounts of work at agreed prices, sharing the proceeds equally amongst the gang. The system was favoured by most contractors as the navvies required only minimal supervision. Between them they had unwittingly presaged the Lump System, scourge of present-day trade unionists in the construction industry. Each butty gang was ruled over by an autocratic headman known as the Butty – after a coal-mine contractor. Of immense physical presence his word was law, any man not pulling his weight in the gang received short shrift from the big man. He was also works convener and negotiator, by nothing more than a cursory inspection of the ground to be worked, and without putting pen to paper he would correctly evaluate the work. Thus belying the belief that brawn and brains cannot go hand in hand.

A total ban on Sunday working played right into the hands of the railway navvy, if he couldn't work he drank. In a drunken stupor with old scores to settle his Sundays became synonymous with fighting and brawling, much to the delight of locals who assembled by the hundred to watch and cheer the bloody encounters.

In June 1838 twenty-five M&L Rly. navvies were locked up and fined 10/- each for drunkenness at Rochdale, and again in August, navvies armed with bludgeons roamed the town knocking down James Wolfenden, one of the town's watchmen. The severely wounded constable being unable to follow his employment, fines of 40/- plus costs were imposed on thirty railway navvies. The exemplary courage of the upholders of law and order, as they strove to restrain the intrusive

wrongdoers, was further demonstrated by an incident at Summit tunnel during late September 1839. David McIntyre, active constable for the Blatchinworth and Calderbrook districts of Littleborough, had gone to the tunnel to arrest an excavator by the name of Donnell. As McIntyre moved forward to apprehend the offender seventy railway navvies stopped work raising their picks and spades on high in a threatening manner. Whereupon the intrepid constable pulled out a brace of pistols, and again advancing said he would "...take the first man who prevented him". The timely intervention of a ganger avoided bloodshed, he explained to the navvies how it would be in everyone's best interest if Donnell was allowed to be taken. McIntyre then made his arrest and escorted the prisoner to the New Bailey lock-ups, Rope Street, Rochdale.

From 1838 – 41 a detachment of the Metropolitan Police Force was stationed at Summit tunnel. As the only body in the country with riot control experience, they were there to assist with any punitive action required to control an affray. It must have been very reassuring for everyone concerned with the upkeep of law and order to know that, until circa 1846 Rochdale had a detachment of soldiers stationed in the town, only 5 miles from the tunnel.

By the expedience of a magistrate reading the Riot Act, upwards of 160 soldiers could have been deployed to put down any disturbance the civil authorities were unable to contain. There is however no evidence of the Riot Act being invoked at the tunnel.

The awesome sight of a platoon of soldiers from Rochdale passing along the turnpike-road in full view of the tunnel surface workers, during November 1838, must have aroused some misgivings of sabre-rattling. As word passed from man to man down the air shafts the truth no doubt became alarmingly distorted. The military were in fact en route to Todmorden, where, without bloodshed, they put down a rampaging mob of over 1,000 textile workers and farm labourers, aided and abetted by railway navvies, in what became known as the Mankinholes Riot.

John Stephenson, was very well acquainted with the Act and riotous assemblies. At Rotherham, while trying to protect his Irish navvies, by herding them to safety into a high walled yard at the back of a public house, he was knocked to the ground by stone throwing English navvies, during the building of the North Midland Railway.

The blasphemous and depraved behaviour of railway navvies, particularly on Sabbath days was strongly contrasted by the order and decorum displayed at the graveside of a fellow worker. Working, eating, sleeping, and drinking together in close proximity inevitably resulted in comradeship, they were after all, as bands of brothers facing a common danger. Yet, most railway navvies were loners whose mateyness proved ephemeral, how could friendships endure between illiterate navvies as eventually they went their separate ways to no fixed abodes? The exceptions were the well-organised Butty Gangs who stayed together for years as travelling companions, working on railway sites throughout the land. Within these tiny combines a staunch camaraderie, unflinching loyalty, and true acts of benevolence were exhibited by the men towards each other. Should one of their gang lose his life, all members without exception attended at the funeral, bareheaded and dressed in their hob-nailed Sunday best.

Standing in total silence with heads bowed, as sober as a row of judges, they astounded all by their demeanour and sobriety. Civilised decency was sometimes shattered when the navvies arrived at a graveyard armed with spades to adjust the grave had it not been dug to their entire satisfaction.

After the internment they would return to their shanty and sell by auction the deceased's worldly possessions, including his most valuable asset, his boots, always assuming that is, they had not been stolen off the corpse. With the monies raised they would proceed to the nearest Ale House to hold a wake. The besotted mourners were unanimous in the belief that only a good send-off would ensure their fallen comrade his rightful place in that celestial palace of the firmament, reserved exclusively for all good railway navvies. By no means were all railway navvies so debauched. At Summit tunnel the spiritual welfare of more sober-minded workers was served by a gift of £30 from the contractor John Stephenson, towards the erection of a church. This would have been a Mission Hall type structure hard by the hutted compound, an interdenominational temporary wooden building of which nothing now remains.

The writer and historian Thomas Carlyle, loathed railway navvies describing them as "... that disorganic mass of labourers". Fortunately his hatred was tempered by the following observations he recorded in a letter written to Gavan Duffy on 29 August 1846.

...the Yorkshire and Lancashire men, I hear are reckoned the worst: and not without glad surprise I find the Irish are best in point of behaviour. The postman tells me that several of the poor Irish do regularly apply to him for money drafts and send their earning home. The English, who eat twice as much beef, consume the residue in whisky and do not trouble the postman.

Money earned in England was indeed used by Irish navvies to pay the rent on their impoverished holdings back in Ireland. Where, unprincipled landlords fully aware of their absentee tenants earning capacity across the water, kept the rents unnaturally high.

The Irish troubles of today are poignantly mirrored in early railway history, when, sectarian indoctrination and sheer ignorance resulted in pitched battles between English, Irish and Scottish navvies. Rather surprisingly there appears to have been a real dearth of Welsh navvies at the time, probably because the only railways operating in Wales up until 1850 were the Chester & Holyhead and Taff Vale railways. Segregation of the warring factions on some lines quite often resulted in unscrupulous contractors using the isolated Irish as cheap labour. Which was extraordinary considering that the gregarious Irish accounted for almost half of all railway navvies working in the north of the country, where, being well-suited to heavy manual work they performed some quite remarkable feats of human endurance.

Irish navvies at work on the M&L Rly. line – many of whom came from Connaught, followed the seasonal migratory route of the hay harvesters and reapers into Great Britain through the port of Liverpool, and followed the line eastward. At Sowerby Bridge, a small group of navvies from the Emerald Isle were attributed with a revival of Roman Catholicism in that area, presumably they married local girls and settled in the town. James Byrne, a politically motivated Irish navvy who undertook to collect a political levy, which was paid with pride by every patriotic Hibernian, in support of the illfated Irish Procursor Society. Byrne was on the line at Todmorden during the summer of 1839 when he wrote that the place was "...among the wild mountains of Yorkshire and more wild Chartists".

The custom of distinguishing peoples ancestry by patronymics was widespread in rural Lancashire at the time. The navvies not wishing to be outdone chose some very descriptive pseudonyms;

Fighting Jack, Gypsy Joe, Long Bob, Canting George, Moleskin Joe and Frying Pan, to name but a few. Men from Lancashire and Yorkshire were identified as Lanky or Yorky, with regional variations ie. Leeds men were known as Woolly Backs. The limbless were accorded little or no consolement with the nomenclature, Wingy. Some navvies were listed in the contractors wage book by their adopted titles, and quite a few deaths recorded using the deceased's byname, or were entered as "a stranger of unknown origin", there being no way of knowing his true identity. At least one navvy forfeited his inheritance in consequence of this practice. Lawyers unable to trace the whereabouts of the man under his proper name distributed £1,000 between other legatees.

Even from this brief account the railway navvy emerges as a complex character with few redeeming qualities. Above all else he was highly skilled in his trade but in other matters backward, gauche and incredibly superstitious. Who else would smash the supposed grave of folk hero Robin Hood, which lay close by the M&L line in Kirklees Park, in the mistaken belief that to carry a small piece as a fetish or luck stone would ward off the toothache? And who decreed that a railway navvy never ever shook hands but would greet a stranger, and take leave of his best mate, with a perfunctory nod of the head? They were however possessed of great compassion, should a man fail to obtain employment on a particular site, he was given a shilling by the on site navvies to sustain him in food and drink as he tramped towards the next railway site. Known as a Navvy's Shilling or Tramping Bob, this charitable act of fraternity was adopted nationally.

The nomadic lifestyle of a railway navvy living rough in open country, his intemperance, poor quality food, and disease, not to mention the sheer hard work, played havoc with his constitution. If still alive at forty he was an old man. In spite of all the suffering and privations there was humour, like the story often related by Robert Stephenson at after dinner speeches. It told of an aggrieved clergyman remonstrating with a group of navvies at the shocking impropriety of working on the Sabbath day, only to be told by the ganger; "Why Soondays aint cropt out ere yet". Or the one about a vicar and his relieved parishioners, who, on completion of a nearby railway line, rang the church bells in celebration of their safe deliverance from a reckless horde of railway navvies.

But the most enduring tale which has gathered the moss of imaginative retelling, and was oft-times told with slight regional variations, concerned a publican's wife who boasted that no mere railway navvy would ever outwit her. The story relates how a young navvy entered her pub carrying a one gallon stoneware bottle and ordered half-a-gallon of gin, which was duly poured into it. They then began to haggle and could not agree as to the cost. Whereupon the landlady ordered the navvy to pour it back which he did, and, without uttering another word left the pub. Unbeknown to the lady the stoneware bottle had contained half-a-gallon of water when he had entered the licensed premises. So they both ended up with a half-gallon of bull, which cost the navvy not a penny.

SHANTYTOWN

It is not too difficult to imagine the plight of young farmworkers in the 1830s, influenced by stories of untold riches leaving their villages and walking phenomenal distances, often hundreds of miles, to find work on the new fangled railways. Only to discover upon arrival there was no accommodation. Of necessity the "sons of the soil" very quickly learned how to put a temporary roof over their heads, eventually becoming as resourceful as the seasoned navvies. Those from the rural north would of course be used to living in such basic accommodation as the scantily furnished Bothies.

When working out in open country, branches torn from trees were laid against the nearest field wall to support a raking roof of turf. The dry-stone wall made windproof with clay. If there was no wall in the vicinity an excavated hollow in the ground would be similarly roofed over. In summertime clustered beads of water dropped from the turf roofs like dewdrops, in winter they froze into icicles. These primitive shelters were the forerunners of what may be loosely described as the railway navvies' lineside homes – The Shanties. Built from whatever material the navvy could lay his hands on, be it borrowed or stolen, they became one of the most striking if sordid manifestations of the early railway scene.

On longer term railway contracts e.g. viaducts and tunnels, it was considered prudent management to provide a limited amount of superior dormitory type accommodation in large wooden sheds. The idea being to maintain a more static workforce, and house key grades of workers in reasonable comfort. The shanties on these sites were also upgraded by the addition of doors, windows, and stovepipes. Roofs were now boarded with timber and made weatherproof with tarred paper, felt, corrugated iron, or tarpaulin sheeting borrowed off a passing goods wagon! The floors remained of compacted earth.

17. *Looking north-east at the site of Summit tunnel shantytown, built around No 7 air shaft. The valley settlement of Warland is seen extreme right*

Accommodation at Summit tunnel consisted of seventy wooden sheds provided by the railway company and 100 shanties built by the navvies themselves. Not a great deal is known about the dormitory units, except that towards the end of the second tunnel contract several of the larger sheds measuring 142ft by 37ft were dismantled and taken to the Summit Tunnel Brickyard, at Featherstall where they were offered for sale. The shanties were concentrated around No 7 air shaft (17) and in Steanor Bottom Wood,where a plentiful supply of rock resulted in substantial stone walled shelters being built, the ruins of which still exist (18). Viewed from high above on Reddyshore Scout Gate packhorse track some of the foundations are seen to describe the symmetrical pattern of terraced dwellings built on opposite sides of a narrow grassy road. Others were apparently divided into "but and ben" type accommodation, for subletting was an essential part of shanty life as a means of making extra money.

A feature common to most railway shantytowns was an open area of level ground set aside from the rustic dwellings. Known as "The Ring" it was the place were wrongs were righted with clenched fists, to the accompanying cheers and jeers of watching navvies, who wagered on the outcome.

18. *Ruins of a navvy built stone shanty*

It would be very wrong to assume that the Summit tunnel shanties sited as they were in splendid rural isolation high on the western shoulder of the Pass, were in any way special or picturesque, they were not. In reality all railway shanties were filthy disease ridden hovels where, "a humane person would hardly put a pig". Where sixty even seventy per cent of the occupants suffered some form of depravation including venereal disease, syphilis was endemic. These overcrowded and unhealthy shacks thrown up arbitrarily and in some haste, without due regard to any Board of Health sanitary regulations, offered little in the way of comfort or decency of living. Herded together in the unwholesome surroundings of closets and stinking middens, where lime-washing was used only as a pesticide, infection spread like wildfire. They very quickly became a putrefying hotbed of disease, in 1837 there was an outbreak of lice borne typhus in the area followed by another at Rotherham one year later. And deadly cholera which had entered the country during 1832 was never very far-away. All in all, things would have been much much worse at Summit, had it not been for a plentiful supply of pellucid drinking water in the Pass. Also, the steeply sloped ground aided dispersal of fetid liquid refuse, which was allowed to flow away from the encampment in open ditches. Nevertheless the malodorous shanties were a microcosm of every social and sanitary ill.

The festering sore of Summit's shantytown was mercifully swept away by time, and the cleansing wind. Today the shanties are all knocked down to their foundation save for a few standing stones, now the habitat of cavorting rabbits. It is a place where ghostly voices of nameless railway navvies moan in the hilltop breeze, echoing the plaintive cry of the curlew. To walk amongst these stone ruins is a highly evocative experience.

As work on any labour intensive railway site peaked, overcrowding in the shanties created its own brand of Rachmanism. In his book *The Railway Navvies*, T Coleman, recalls how some unscrupulous shanty keepers charged extortionate rents – fourpence a night for a bed, one penny to sleep on a table, to shake down on the floor one-halfpenny.

Making maximum use of the available floor space trundle-beds were used, and children slept suspended from the roof in baskets, known in navvy slang somewhat appropriately as Brat Cages. Peter Thompson, a railway contractor with a social conscience, had the foresight to design and build the "Labourers Moral Cottage" so named because it segregated the sexes. Sectionally built in stud framed units with corrugated iron roofs they could be dismantled and re-erected at will – the first prefabs? At rather less than £65 each they were not popular, and considered far too expensive by most contractors. The navvies no doubt reasoned that by building their own shacks they would pay no rent at all.

Missionaries reported that the only reading matter to be found in a railway shanty township was; the freely distributed mission bible, *Lloyds Weekly Newspaper*, and copies of the *Illustrated Police News*, from which pictures of wanted criminals were displayed on the shanty walls. To most people the interior of a navvy built shanty was a complete mystery, and would have remained so had it not been for one man writing in later life about his railway experiences in the magazine *Household Words*, a weekly periodical published by the author Charles Dickens.

He describes what it was really like to live in a railway shanty, his lucid text evokes the sordid lifestyle to a tee. Unfortunately Dickens had decreed that all contributed articles published in his magazine should appear anonymously, save those penned by the literary master himself. Thus, the railway contributor was condemned to unacknowledged obscurity, which is more the pity considering that he was a well-informed competent writer.

He recounts how in 1835 as a lad of sixteen with aspirations of becoming an engineer he ran away from home to work on the railway. First, as a tip truck driver from which he was sacked for driving his horse and tip truck down an embankment, later he worked as a bucket-steerer at an air shaft. Being of smart appearance in his clean clothes the on site navvies christened him Dandy

Dick. With no thanks to C D that is how we too must remember the anonymous author of the following admirable piece of railway history.

Dandy Dick lived in a small shanty from where he was able to observe with increasing incredulity, the antics and lifestyle of a twenty man butty gang living communally in a large shanty, presided over by an old crone named Peg. In charge of all the domestic arrangements the hag was expected to cook, wash, mend, clean, and make the beds. In addition to which, being privy to every conceivable obscenity, she would occasionally lend a hand with the infighting, to which her two black eyes and heavily bandaged chin bore painful witness.

Only once was the lad given leave to enter the "den of the wild men" as he called the shanty. Having offered to teach one of their members how to read, he approached the tarpaulin roofed shanty one wet Sunday morning in May. After old Peg had cursed him in a manner intended to be friendly she told Dandy Dick his pupil George was out, but to sit down and wait, as he would be back shortly,which the lad did on a three-legged stool near the door. With the keen eye of youth the lad missed nothing as he looked about the shanty. Being the day of rest most of the occupants were at home, some in bed asleep or drunk, each recumbent trusting no-one used his kitbag for a pillow. Others sat about talking, smoking or drinking, they offered the lad a beer but he declined, two lay outstretched on the floor playing cards, another sat astride a stool repairing his boots. In amongst the men were several dogs with litters of puppies of the Bull Terrier and Lurcher breeds, the one used for fighting the other for poaching.

Next to the window were three large barrels of beer, on tap but all securely padlocked, the keys for which hung from a leather girdle around Peg's thick waist, for she was also appointed tapster. The opposite end of the one roomed shanty served as kitchen-cum-eating area, there on a rickety wooden table plates of tin, wood and earthenware were spread about along with an odd assortment of chipped cups, bowls, basins, and cutlery, nothing matched. In one corner stood a rude dresser and a double row of rough wooden cupboards used as tommy boxes, one allotted to each man. Hanging on the wall over a central fireplace the lad counted a dozen or so of the navvies' guns.

In the opposite corner old Peg was busying herself placing coals on a fire under a large copper boiler, from which a cloud of savoury steam escaped. Several strings emerged from the vapour each attached to a piece of wood, somewhat puzzled the lad asked what they were for.

> "Them"! said Peg speaking in a broad Lancashire dialect, and taking a stick in her hands, "Why, sith'ee lad, this bit o'stick has four nicks ont, well it's Billygoats dinner, he's a-bed yond, now this", taking up another with six nicks; "is that divil Redhead's and this", seizing a third with ten nicks "is Happy Jacks, well thee knowest he's got a bit o'beef; Redheads nowt but taters, he's a gradely brute is Redhead! and Billygoats got a pun or so o'bacon an' a cabbage. Now thee sees, I've a matter o'twenty dinners or so to bile every day which I biles in nets, an if I dinna' fix em i this road, I sud ha'niver tell where to find em, and there'ud be sich a row as niver yet was heer'd on".

Old Peg was typical of that unfortunate class of skivvy who worked amongst the railway navvies, providing some semblance of creature comforts for their rough masters. Work that was as hard as it was unrewarding. Younger women of easy virtue doubled as unpaid shanty keepers, tally-women and concubines, giving birth to their bastard offspring. What *married* couples there were; many lived over the brush. Chadwick wrote "... at their wedding the couple jumped over a broomstick in a room full of men, and were put to bed at once in the same room." Most men in the camps were young and womanless, for navvying was never conducive to conjugal bliss, in any case like Jack Tar the footloose nomads much preferred to love em and leave em.

Shanty women like their menfolk adopted a distinctive style of dress, they wore black bonnets decorated with brightly coloured penny ribbons, muslin frocks, linsey undergarments, and thick leather boots. Cheap earrings and necklaces, mere baubles, appear to have been an obligatory gimcrack adornment. All could swear like a trooper and many drank to excess. One observant shanty watcher noted that those women smoking short clay pipes were usually slatterns who lived in squalor, whilst the ones using long church-warden pipes were always neat and tidy about themselves, and kept a clean shanty.

The navvies secular lifestyle shocked the Victorian concept of Christian morality to its very core. But what could be done with such profane infidels who only spoke of God to wonder why he had made some so poor and others rich, and who loaned or sold their common-law wives, and Mission Bibles for beer money? The answer was very little.

At the very beginning of the railway era sporadic attempts to convert the sinners by people of Nonconformist persuasion had only limited success. Over thirty-years were to elapse before missionary work amongst the railway navvies got properly organised with the founding by Revd. Lewis Moules Evans of the Navvy Mission Society, and Elizabeth Garnett's less successful Christian Excavators Union.

Both were formed on work sites near Leeds, the Revd. Evans said his was the direct result of a conversation he had with a navvy in a third-class railway carriage somewhere in the north of England. But it must be said most railway navvies cared not one jot about the fulminations of religious zealots, they were there for the money and precious little else. Salvation to them was in finding another job immediately one contract finished, to keep the merry-go-round of eating, drinking, and sleeping in motion. At heart they were as showmen enjoying the notoriety, knowing they were different from other mortals they played the part just that little larger than life, if only to antagonise the do-gooders.

Having distanced themselves from populated areas, normal social contacts, and the moral control of family life, trusting no-one save their immediate confidants the shanty dwellers were seen as – an encamped horde of rogues, picaroons, and vagabonds, or worse, as latter-day anarchists, and Chartists with whores. In point of fact the enclaves appear to have been well-conducted in a rough-and-ready sort of way, as was every aspect of a railway navvy's working life. Governed by a sort of fraternal working mans freemasonry, an unwritten code of practice existed with rules and regulations upheld by the fist. Taboos the uneducated confrerie willingly accepted, and obeyed to further and protect their working lives.

So a legend was born, a myth hastened by rumour and ignorance that portrayed the railway navvy as a blasphemous heathen, social misfit, and bogeyman all rolled into one. Of course it was never quite so simplistic, things rarely are, but his reputation went before him, and many a naughty Victorian child was chided by the admonition "behave yerself or I'll give yer to a navvy".

Co-op & Tommy Shops

The book *Snapshots From The History of Littleborough*, a compilation of newspaper articles written by F Jackson, records the extraordinary supposition that the co-operative movement originated at Summit close by the tunnel:

> an old Smithy Nook resident Mr Thomas Stansfield[1] always maintained that co-operation started there and not in Rochdale. He said during the railway era 1837-8 several of them joined together and took a house at Stoneyroyd[2] bought goods wholesale and sold them out retail to members. He used to wax very indignant when he spoke about it that Rochdale should claim the honour.
>
> *(1) also identified as Thomas Schofield.*
> *(2) perhaps Stoney Field or Stoney Head.*

Although work on the M&L Rly. did in fact predate by seven years the opening of the Rochdale Society of Equitable Pioneers famous shop at No 31 Toad Lane on 21 December 1844, there had been previous attempts at forming co-operatives in the town. In 1833 a co-operative shop at 15 Toad Lane failed within 2 years because of unrecovered debts. Prior to which an embryotic co-operative involved with the sale of flannel goods operated for a time in Rochdale around 1830, and there were many more throughout the country. The Rochdale Pioneers, – they later changed their name to Rochdale Equitable Pioneers Society Ltd. – place in history is, as its name implies, as the worlds first *successful* co-operative society having perfected, but did not invent, the payment of dividend upon purchases. Within seven-years there were over 130 Co-operative Societies operating on the Rochdale principle, by the turn of the century it was a world-wide organisation.

Nevertheless Jackson's reputed claimant cannot be dismissed lightly, for although we may never know what really transpired at Stoneyroyd the fact that it coincided with the railway era, and occurred near a major railway site is very significant. Bulk-buying and retailing of consumer goods at or near railway building sites is an undisputed fact, regrettable it was for reasons very far removed from the ideals of co-operation. Operated by the railway contractor as a highly profitable sideline through retail outlets known variously as: Tommy, Truck, Tick, or Badger Shops. The system, a variant of the infamous Truck System was used to rob, cheat, and swindle the railway navvy of his hard earned money. Many a contractor recouped heavy losses incurred on an underpriced contract by operating the system.

On the face of it Tommy Shops at railway sites was to be recommended, as a timely solution to a difficult problem, or so it appeared. With navvies living alongside the track quite often in remote areas with no access to shops, it seemed prudent management that a contractor should elect to purchase consumer goods wholesale, bring them up the line and retail them at the work site – but that was where the rackets started.

The system, which began during the canal building era, flourished because of the workers inability to handle money wisely, and his immoderate use of intoxicating liquor. With wages paid monthly or even longer, at the first Woodhead tunnel navvies were paid at intervals of nine weeks. The accumulated earnings were just too much of a temptation for the weak-willed labourers. With pockets jingling they would down tools on payday to go on a bacchanalian spree of hard drinking day and night. Not until funds ran out would they even contemplate returning to work.

The contractor, knowing that after every payday many working days would be lost, was obliged to adjust his monthly work schedules accordingly. Acutely aware of these problems the M&L directors had three new clauses written into the second tunnel contract, designed specifically to counter the serious disruptions resulting from alcoholic addiction.

1. John Stephenson was instructed to pay his men fortnightly.

2. Disbursement of earnings to be at a place within a half-mile of the tunnel.

3. The contractor was forbidden to erect any Beer or Gin Shops at the tunnel without the written consent of three M&L Rly. Co. directors.

The previously noted interim payments made to the contractor, enabled him to comply with the first clause. With wages invariably paid out at the nearest public house on Saturdays the second clause also presented no great problems at Summit. The third, however must have brought a wry smile to the face of John Stephenson, a contractor of his calibre would never have contemplated such a proposition. In any case the district abounded with people only too willing to provide the navvy with his sublime beverage at beer shops, ale houses, public houses and hush houses – low beer shops quite often unlicensed.

At Doghills, Boniface Samuel Uttley owned and operated a Beer Shop & Brew-House ideally situated to quench the thirst of navvies working in the deepest shafts. It must remain a matter of some conjecture just how many flagons of his home-brew were lowered down No 3½ shaft (sited across the road from the brew-house) during the protracted struggle to sink that most difficult of all shafts. At Summit, only a matter of yards from the tunnel entrance one Charles Kershaw plied his dual trade as brewster/pig breeder, no doubt supplying jugs of ale and bacon callops to the hungry navvies. Like many another 1830s brew-house that particular establishment at No 3 Rock Nook, Summit, later burgeoned into a fully licensed hostelry "The Rock Tavern". A public house created by the needs and requirements of railway builders it no longer exists.

Unlike the earlier Summit Inn at the opposite end of the village, which also prospered during the railway age and still functions, under a new name "The Summit".

Although the eighteenth century expression, "Drunk for a penny, dead-drunk for twoppence", could never be levelled against more highly paid artisans of a later age, it speaks volumes for the potency of family brewed double hopped ale. The more addicted railway navvies remained permanently under the influence of this strong drink, going to work pot-valourous, glassy eyed, and befuddled, a danger to themselves and everyone about them, but convinced that:

Shallow draughts intoxicate the brain,
And drinking largely sobers us again.
                              Alexander Pope

With Britain on the verge of famine due in no small measure to the infamous Corn Laws, food was expensively inadequate and wages low, drink was the only solace for the toiling masses. It was against this background that seven enlightened men in Preston Lancashire "signed the pledge" in 1832 heralding the start of Teetotalism. Despite scorn and much ridicule they soldiered on, the movement eventually achieving some degree of success through Temperance Societies, Rechabites, Good Templers, Bands of Hope etc etc. The railway navvy, suffering from alcoholic melancholy, was of course blissfully oblivious to such abstemious activities however well-intentioned they were. Having spent all his earnings on "thoughtless folly and the sad love of drink" the navvy had perforce to survive on credit until the next payday.

This he did by obtaining a voucher or ticket from his ganger, which entitled him to purchase goods at the on site Tommy Shop up to the value of the ticket, the total credit being duly deducted from his next wage. That piece of paper was of course non-negotiable redeemable only at the on site Tommy Shop, where the consumer goods on offer were of a very inferior quality; poor bacon, rancid butter, meat from cheapest cuts, watered-down beer etc was the norm, and all at exorbitant prices. The out of funds navvy had no choice; he bought there or starved.

During 1846 a Parliamentary Select Committee sat for eight-days under the chairmanship of the Hon Edward Pleydell Bouverie, member for Kilmarnock, to study the working conditions of railway navvies. It was told by one witness, the Revd J R Thompson, that the men paid thirty per cent over the odds for food bought at Tommy Shops – and that was only the beginning of racketeering.

The navvy's own ganger started the fiddles by imposing a surcharge of ten per cent on every ticket obtained from the contractors office. With it the navvy had three options and was on a loser whichever he chose. He could; obtain food at extortionate prices from the Tommy Shop. Or he could use it to buy beer at a local pub, where a 4/- ticket would be worth only 2/6d – the publican wanted his cut too. As a last resort it could occasionally be exchanged for coin of the realm, when the navvy was fortunate to receive half its value. A sardonic comment by an anonymous navvy says it all. "… they give us great wages but they take it all from us again".

There can be no doubt about it, with the arrival of John Stephenson at Summit, and the strictures imposed by the M&L Rly. Co. in the second tunnel contract, the catering arrangements improved tenfold. Profiteering was stopped and with money in his pocket the navvy was free to choose where he obtained his provisions.

The sole concern of a good company railway engineer was uninterrupted progress of the work in hand by a contented workforce – a contented navvy being a well-victualled one. Where he obtained his provisions was no concern of the engineer, if the Truck System was in operation he turned a blind eye to it. Should a contractor cease trading and the on site Tommy Shop close, the engineers would hurriedly assume tutelage for the navvies welfare, and make alternative arrangements for the purveyance of food. This they did by detailing the subengineers to call on every shopkeeper in the area advising them of the numbers employed on site, in the expectation that stocks would be increased. One can imagine how the more entrepreneurial Littleborough retailers responded to the call and became part-time Sutlers, trundling handcarts around the shanties with a daily supply of meat and freshly baked bread. But however it was achieved, the feeding of over 1,000 men in the hutted compound and hilltop shanties at Summit tunnel in what was after all a sparsely populated area, was an outstanding logistical achievement.

An 1846 Select Committee had recommended that the Truck Acts of 1831, which abolished the system in factories be extended to include railway construction sites. This was ignored by Parliament, primarily because of sitting members vested interests – the majority were share-holders, and one seventh directors of railway companies. At Summit tunnel conditions had improved dramatically, but elsewhere the iniquitous system rolled on robbing and cheating the gullible navvy, until the Truck Amendment Act of 1887 finally outlawed it. By which time the countrywide railway network was nearing completion and the largest nomadic workforce the country had witnessed was, as an effective force in decline. At the turn of the century the legion armies of railway navvies had for the most part passed into history, or as they themselves would have put it in navvy slang they just – "sloped off".

7. Daring Disabled or Dead

On Saturday 17 August 1985, Todmorden Round Table organised a highly successful charity walk through Summit tunnel (19) just two days before it reopened following the disastrous fire which engulfed the central part of the tunnel. Extensive and expensive repairs had closed the tunnel for a period of eight-months. Of the 5,500 people who paid £1 each for the privilege of walking through a continuously illuminated, airy, and reasonably dry tunnel, none could possibly have imagined the scene 150 years earlier. When hundreds of workers suffered injury, sickness, and death during the building of that Pennine hell-hole.

19. *Start of Todmorden Round Table charity walk through Summit tunnel 17 August 1985*

The appalling casualty figures were by no means singular, and to a degree a high incidence of personal injury would have been accepted as inevitable, for tunnelling was and still is a highly dangerous occupation. The large number of fatalities was quite another matter. Many high-ranking M&L officials very conveniently subscribed to a widely held belief that the high death rate was, the result of carelessness, inexperience, derring do, and the devil-may-care attitude of the navvies themselves. Mr J D Barry, of the Associated Contractors Office in Man-

chester, stated in a letter to the *Manchester Guardian*, that John Stephenson preferred to pick steady, sober, moral men whom he would train and promote, rather than employ more experienced tunnellers, who tended to be drunken and dissolute. A statement partially corroborated by the recorded death of a sixteen-year-old lad, the youngest tunnel casualty.

In these more safety conscious times we are told by the Health & Safety Executive that accidents do not just happen, but are caused by human error, and are therefore preventable. A maxim which could have been put to good effect in the air shafts at Summit tunnel, where the first fatal accident occurred on 19 February 1838, when all the shafts were comparatively shallow, and had increased alarmingly as they deepened.

By October 1839 sixteen deaths had been officially recorded, of which five occurred within an eight-day period during September – the blackest month.

5 September
> As two labourers were being lowered by hand operated winch down the 201ft deep No 4 air shaft to carry out emergency repairs to a damaged air pipe, the winding mechanism pawl slipped out of gear precipitating both men to the bottom of the shaft. One falling amongst the timbers died instantly, the other drowned in the shaft sump.

6 September
> When a youth was lowering a tub of spoil onto a sliding section of tramway he had pushed over the shaft head, it accidentally became unlatched and began to move under him. Losing his balance the hapless navvy plunged headlong to his death down the shaft.

11 September
> Roger Warrin, a miner, killed in tunnel explosion.

12 September
> Ascending the deepest shaft seated astride a loaded tub of spoil (surely a blatant breach of regulations) a young navvy had almost gained the surface when the swaying tub struck the shaft wall casting him to certain death 310ft below. This accident confirms that guides similar to those used in coalmines to prevent tubs from swinging and spiralling during winding were not used at Summit tunnel.

The Rochdale & District Coroner, Thomas Ferrand Dearden, held a court of inquest into these deaths over three of the bodies at the Summit Inn. Verdicts of accidental death were recorded, with an addendum that a deodand of £5 be exacted in respect of the machinery for each life lost in No 4 air shaft.

Deodand – an old English Statute, which by common law required any personal goods or chattels, or in the case of machinery its value, which had accidentally caused the death of a human being to be assigned Deo Dandum (to be given to God). Which was achieved by forfeiture to the Crown for pious uses, monies collected were usually expended as alms to the families of the deceased, the Act was repealed 1846. William Robertson, the Rochdale writer and historian, recorded Deodands to a total value of £36 12s 03d in respect of ten lives lost during the building of Summit tunnel. Which confirms that only one-quarter of the fatalities were attributable to machinery failure.

Alarmed at the spate of accidents the Board instructed its tunnel engineers to report fully on the cause of all major accidents. It also appointed one of its directors to attend at every coroners inquest, with a view to guarding against any recurrence. But it was all to no avail, carnage in the air shafts seemed never ending; on Thursday 23 January 1840 two more men were killed and five seriously injured by a partial collapse in No 1½ shaft at Temple Lane.

When maximum output was achieved at the tunnel during late 1839, almost 500 men and boys were at work below ground at any one time, all were at risk. Within the tunnel cavity the real danger was of course gunpowder, or to be more precise, blackpowder, as the shot was called. Equally unstable it differed in formulation from that used as a propellant charge by the army and navy of the period. Accidents sustained during the firing of explosive charges could, and should, have been considerably reduced by the use of a new safety fuse which was readily available. Invented by William Bickford of Tuckingmill, Cornwall, the patent slow burning fuse allowed more accurate firing of the shot. Alas, most contractors considered it to be far too expensive, and by the bonus conscious miners far too slow. Judging by the numerous references to accidents caused by premature detonation it would appear not to have been used at Summit tunnel. The alternative was simply, effective, but highly dangerous.

After the blackpowder had been poured into the

drill hole – about a pint or "two tots" as a measure was called – would usually suffice in limestone, a pricker was inserted before the hole was tamped with clay using a stemming bar. The pricker was then withdrawn and substituted by a straw filled with priming powder. The firing of this improvised fuse was very much a hit-or-miss affair, the shot-firer did not always have enough time to race towards a safe refuge before the explosion shattered the rock-face hurling debris in all directions. Another frequent cause of accidents involved the use of iron stemming bars (ramrods) when charging the drill holes. Should the stemmer accidentally strike the side of the hole causing a spark, the charge was prematurely ignited, propelling the stemming bar at high velocity from its rocky cavern into the miner's body. That particular problem was solved by the use of copper stemming bars.

The unfortunate death of Roger Warrin in Summit tunnel made apparent the vulnerability of all face-workers as they went about their dangerous tasks. At work in a heading where several explosive charges had been set and ignited, Warrin had retreated some 60yd from the rock-face, further than any of his workmates, yet was the only casualty of a fourteen man gang. Struck on the head by a fragment of rock he died instantly. At the time of his demise Roger Warrin was the only married man to lose his life in Summit tunnel, leaving a wife and three children. A belated sequel to this sad affair was exhibited when Captain Laws RN superintendent of the line, himself a qualified civil engineer, sent detailed drawings to the tunnel engineers of a portable protective shield of his own design to be used during blasting.

Even drilling the shot hole could be fraught with danger. The drill, a short iron bar, was held with both hands and slowly rotated by one man, while being struck in rapid succession by two men wielding heavy hammers. It was said that the man holding the drill – he was known as a "Shaker", rarely suffered superficial injury, for if accidentally hit by the flying hammers the blow usually proved fatal. The Shaker's precarious occupation giving rise to the humourous epigram "when I nod my head hit it".

Using this method of drilling, a shot hole in limestone could be sunk to a depth of 12in in half-an-hour. The much longer "Jumper" drill struck by three well co-ordinated hammers was used less frequently in tunnels because of the confined space. Resident blacksmiths were kept busy drawing out and resharpening the square bevelled chisels.

If working underground was of necessity claustrophobic it was also damp and foul smelling. To which an admixture of gunpowder smoke, nonexistent sanitation, unwashed flesh and the beery exhalations of railway navvies stripped to the waist, leaves little to be imagined. In such unhealthy confines it was imperative to provide a good supply of clean fresh air to the nethermost regions of the tunnel. It was achieved by installing large fans at the top of each air shaft. Housed in metal cowlings the fans were belt driven from the stationary winding engines. For some obscure reason each fan was referred to by the navvies as a "Blow George".

The air was blown through 12in diameter sheet metal tubing which passed down the air shafts, where they were frequently crushed during winding operations. Within the tunnel the tubes were extended forward into the heading with each advance. For a short distance behind each heading a movable wooden framed partition covered with strong tarred cloth, known as a brattice, divided the tunnel longitudinally into two equal parts. By blowing fresh air down one side of the brattice, foul air was forced out of the heading along the opposite section, to be dispersed up the nearest air shaft. A much older, but nonetheless effective method of tunnel ventilation, was that of lowering fire-baskets down to the bottom of air shafts. Rising currents of warm air in the shafts drew pungent odours out of the heading.

Temperature in a tunnel heading of average depth remained constant at a stifling damp 80°F 26°C until two headings were joined by driftway. Ventilation then became relatively easy, with one shaft designated "upcast" and the other a "down-cast" shaft movement of air became more controllable. Working conditions however became decidedly draughty and the temperature plumm-eted to 55°F 13°C.

As the intrepid miners toiled for their meagre share of that pot of gold the Railway Nabobs were serving up, most were fully cognisant of the terrible risks involved. Explosions, roof-falls, and perpetual dampness enveloped them, conditions which caused those men past the first flush of youth to suffer from rheumatics. All were perhaps blissfully unaware of other more insidious perils that beset them. As charge after explosive charge blasted the Summit hillside filling the tunnel cavity with a pervasive cloud of thick sulphurous smoke, which often took well over an hour to clear, the miner was at his most vulnerable. Prolonged inhalation of smoke and dust resulted in various pulmonary disorders, bronchitis, wracking coughs, and the occupational disease silicosis. The dietary disease scurvy also took its toll, and was for a time renamed the "railway disease", added to which debilitating dysentery, and degenerative consumption also caused much suffering. All in all not a very congenial working environment even for the strongest of men.

S T S & B B S

But help was at hand and it came just at the right time, in late August 1839, only a matter of days before the succession of accidents during black September. To alleviate the sufferings and privations his men were having to endure John Stephenson, aided by Barnard Dickinson, established a workers benefit society at the tunnel. Although the Summit Tunnel Sickness & Burial Benefit Society was constituted and functioned as a self-financing charitable found-ation, it was inaugurated by liberal endowments donated by the directors of the M&L Rly. Co. and John Stephenson.

The Society operated under the stewardship of two paid officials, a secretary/treasurer and a resident surgeon, Dr Barker, who received £20 monthly for his services. Travis, records that John Barker MD lived and practised in Little-borough, presumably his secondment as tunnel medic proved a lucrative adjunct to his work as the village doctor. What tales the learned doctor could have told about Summit tunnel shanty-town, and its occupants, had he only put pen to paper.

Every workman subscribed 6d weekly from his wages to the Society funds, which entitled him to full medical and surgical treatment, in all cases of sickness or injury. Should a member become incapacitated he received 10/- weekly until fit and strong enough to resume work. If at the doctor's discretion a patient's lodgings was not considered to be conducive towards a speedy recovery the sufferer was, "conveyed to an hospital provided expressly for the purpose", where he received every attention.

The hospital would most probably have been a temporary wooden building set apart from the hutted compound, with perhaps four or six beds, – but infinitely more comfortable than shantytown.

In all cases of death, funeral expenses were defrayed by the Society, plus a lump sum payment to dependant relatives, the amount determined by individual needs and circumstances was calculated over and above a £15 minimum grant. This was indeed a mighty leap forward, previous to the setting up of the Sickness fund it had been customary, in the event of a fatal accident, for the deceased's workmates to pay 1/- each to the contractor to cover funeral expenses. Life was particularly hard for those he left behind, the superstitious navvies, believing an on site unattached woman to be the foreboder of ill-omens saw to it that the deceased's tally-woman and her illegitimate brats vacated the commune forthwith. The empty shanty would be taken over by a working but homeless navvy. Dispossessed, penniless, and hungry the banished woman and her brood then had two options, she could; shack up with another navvy, thus perpetuating her sordid lifestyle, or be "thrown on the parish as paupers". It was rough justice for a young woman who had given her best, but rules were rules, that was the way things were.

By December 1840 no less than £2,024 3s 11d had been subscribed to the STS&BBS over a seventy-one week period, which averaged 1,147 weekly subscriptions. Figures that show it to have been a broad based society with a full membership. After extolling its virtues and recommending the institution as an example worthy of imitation on other works of magnitude a newspaper report concluded with:

> ...It is almost needless to add, that this institution has proved a great blessing to the workmen who belong to a class but ill prepared to meet a season of sickness and its concomitant needs and privations.

That season of sickness at Summit tunnel had been both long and hard, within two-months of the Society being wound up 1,507 men and boys had received medical attention of one kind or another. From simple cuts, lacerations, dislocations, contusions, to the more serious cases of horrific burns incurred during blasting, and loss of limbs from roof falls. The brain child of John Stephenson the STS&BBS had proved as imaginative in concept as it was fortuitous in bringing timely relief to the long-suffering workforce.

Friendly Societies had been proliferating in southeast Lancashire since 1815 as provident insurance against a rainy day, and also to counter the appalling sufferings endured by the mal-treated lower classes. It was therefore not all that exceptional to discover a system of social self-help operating at Summit tunnel during 1839-41.

Within twelve months of its completion the tunnel casualty list was being questioned, it came in the form of a letter written to a newspaper editor. In it the writer, who lived in Summit Village, purports to enumerate the various causes of accidental deaths.

Summit Tunnel

To the Editor of the *Manchester Guardian*

Gentlemen – Knowing that you have taken a lively interest in the difficult and dangerous works of the Manchester and Leeds Railway, I am induced to beg you will publish the following remarks in reference to the Summit Tunnel in your excellent paper.

At the opening of the Shildon Tunnel near Bishop Auckland reported in the *Durham Chronicle* on the 14 Jan last a Mr Booth in responding to the toast given by Mr Storey to the contractors, said; – "Before he came to the Shildon Tunnel he was engaged with a tunnel on the Manchester & Leeds Railway, and upon it he was sorry to say that more than forty individuals lost their lives".

I do remember a person of the name of Booth obtaining employment as a banksman or timekeeper from one of the contractors of the Summit tunnel; but the statement he has made is grossly exaggerated. I am sorry to say there were eight lives lost in the tunnel by shots going off prematurely, by falling materials, and in the shafts, eleven by negligence and carelessness, five by the failure of machinery, and four at the bottoms of the shafts by falling materials; in all twenty eight individuals who lost their lives in this great undertaking by accidents, and two men died in the hospital from natural causes – I am gentlemen, your obedient servant

Richard Taylor
Summit 14 Feb 1842

In the absence of firm documentary evidence such detailed information must remain purely conjectural, the letter also contains two serious discrepancies, viz – lives lost in the air shafts was considerably higher than the collective number quoted, and deaths attributable to machinery failure is well-documented at ten, not five. It is however historically significant that the writer also lists negligence and carelessness as the prime cause of death, and confirms the existence of a hospital.

The rapid rise in status of the man Henry Booth, from that of Banksman at Summit tunnel to principal contractor at the Shildon tunnel, was the direct result of marital ties pledged at Summit, Booth having married the daughter of the tunnels first contractor James Copeland. Upon his release from debtors prison in 1840 Copeland straightway resumed his career as a railway contractor at the Shildon tunnel, whereupon Booth left Summit tunnel and went to work for his father-in-law. During the following year after a brief illness James Copeland died, and Henry Booth was invited by the directors of that line to finish the contract.

To fully comprehend the horrendous chapter of accidents at Summit tunnel two attendant factors must be considered, firstly the numbers of lives lost was not pro rata to tunnel length. This was precisely the point Henry Booth was making in his speech at the opening of the 3/4 mile long Shildon tunnel, where only five men died. And which he contrasted with the 2,885yd long Summit tunnel toll of forty-one lives lost, implying that a tunnel could be classified good or bad by the efficiency of its construction management. The other dominant factor, in this sorry tale of human suffering, is concerned with an ever recurring reference to negligence and carelessness resulting from ineptitude amongst railway navvies themselves. For whatever reasons, be they financial or altruistic, the declared preference of John Stephenson to employ only "steady sober, moral men" at the tunnel, knowing them to be inexperienced tunnellers and therefore at risk, must rank as the major contributory cause of death.

In a paper read before the Statistical Society of Manchester during 1846 Sir Edwin Chadwick, the eminent social reformer, disclosed that on a percentage basis more men died in Summit Tunnel (sic) than were killed in the battles of Salamanca, Vittoria, Talavera and Waterloo. Adding that only 2.11 per cent of the soldiers were killed at Waterloo, compared with a tunnel mortality rate of 3 per cent. He was of course referring to the first Woodhead tunnel 5,300 yd on the Manchester Sheffield & Lincolnshire line, where thirty-three men died and 200 were severely injured within the tunnel and its disease ridden navvy shanty encampment on Pikenaze Moor, where a number died of cholera.

Nevertheless Chadwick's oratory makes a fitting analogy to what happened at the real Summit tunnel, where far more deaths and injuries occurred. Writing in 1876, within living memory of the great undertaking, William Robertson of Rochdale recorded the deaths of forty-one men and boys at Summit tunnel, which averaged one human life sacrificed for each 70yd of completed tunnel.

No graven list of names on some spurious obelisk exists to chronicle their passing, for in life they were persons of little or no account, in death they are forgotten. The great tunnel they helped to build must stand as a fitting memorial to the forty-one souls who gave their lives that we may pass in safety.

8. TOWARDS THE SUMMIT OF ATTAINMENT

THE PERMANENT WAY

As the year 1840 wore on work at Summit passed its peak, as segmented sections of tunnel were joined to form one long continuous cavity and made ready for laying the permanent way. The workforce had been drastically scaled down to a few hundred men who would carry out this work.

Redundant railway navvies carrying their scant possessions set out on foot from Summit, in search of other railway work. Those still in funds enjoyed the rare privilege of travelling on the railway they helped to build, as far as Manchester. Most were heading for the Chorley and Blackburn areas, where many found employment, the skilled tunnellers working for their old employer. After Summit John Stephenson was invited, or *implored*, to complete the immensely difficult Chorley tunnel.

At least one local family followed the mass egress, Jackson relates how members of the Yates household, having worked at the tunnel obtained railway work at Blackburn. Conversely a few navvies stayed on and settled in the area, some of the newcomers integration into the community being mutually beneficial. Although Jackson comments, "...others were of a more undesirable character and helped considerably in lowering the tone of morality in the village". Not an entirely unexpected turn of events, considering the hilltop shanties had ensconced a horde of drunken hell raisers whose urbanism would have been a protracted process.

Above ground all the winding-engines, boilers, and fire-holes were dismantled save one, at No 7 air shaft the winding gear was retained in full working order until final completion, the reason was twofold; Its central position in the tunnel, and a plentiful supply of rock on the surface near the shaft. Which, when broken and mixed with soil was used as ballast infill, upon which the permanent way was laid. On an elevated wooden platform erected at the bottom of No 7 shaft the ballast was stockpiled, prior to being delivered to all parts of the tunnel.

Bold in concept, daring in its execution, and stupendous to behold, the Manchster & Leeds Railway was all of that and more, with one very significant exception – the original permanent way was a total disaster. The engineer-in-chief's obsession with stone block sleepers was to cost the company dearly.

An inveterate *conservative* in every sense of the word George Stephenson's career at the time of Summit was being rapidly overtaken by events. As the galloping progress of railway technology raced ahead at an unprecedented rate, the old engineer clung tenaciously to past outmoded tenets. His dogged adherence to the problematic track was wholly indefensible, considering its one and only benefit was a clear bridle-path between the rails. A facility rendered obsolete by his own proven superiority of steam locomotion over horse-traction, with his famous locomotive *Rocket* in 1829. He was however not alone in the misconception, his own son Robert, J Locke, I K Brunel, and many others had to learn the hard way that, in order to avoid loose rivets, and broken axles, a track required to be carefully ballasted. Disregarding what was so patently obvious George Stephenson stubbornly insisted that his track be fastened down rock solid to *terra firma*, using 2ft square blocks of stone to achieve that end. Weighing $\frac{1}{4}$ ton each and set diagonally at 3ft centres, they were used at the rate of 7,040 blocks per single mile of double track.

Each stone block was bedded by repeatedly raising it off the ground with a spring lever, and allowing it to fall until its base was solid and flattened. The fall distance and resultant ground compaction, was calculated to be consistent with the weight of a train passing over the stone block. It was also claimed that by setting the blocks diagonally instead of at right angles to the rail (20), they countered the horizontal thrust of a moving train. And were more easily reset by side ramming should they become dislodged. Some stone blocks were purchased from local quarries, but most came from excavations along the line, the most productive being the deep cutting between Elland and Brighouse.

20. *Robert Stephenson type 2-2-2 locomotive passing platelayers at work laying stone block sleepers near Hebden Bridge during 1840s*

Malleable iron rails of single parallel form weighing 56lbs per yard, were laid in lengths of 15ft to a gauge of 4ft 9in this was half-an-inch wider than the Liverpool & Manchester Rly. lines to which they were subsequently joined. The rails were secured in chairs by ball and key (t), the chairs being spiked into oak tree-nails set in 1³/₄in diameter holes drilled in the stone blocks. The only concession towards cushioning being a permeated piece of felt interposed between chair and stone block.

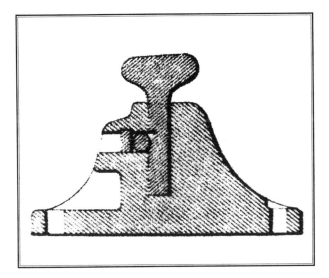

T. *Original M&L Rly. ball and key chair with T-section rail*

Prohibitively expensive to maintain and extremely uncomfortable to ride upon, the ironroad very quickly began to fail. As the blocks inevitably subsided or tilted, undulations along the lines horizontal plane created a wave effect, causing a train to judder and sway. And, without transverse ties the gauge varied alarmingly, resulting in derailments, accidents, even deaths. By 1844, only three-years after the line opened throughout, work began removing tens of thousands of stone blocks. Replacing them with a more resilient track comprising of wooden sleepers correctly ballasted, and a much heavier rail. The redundant stone blocks were stockpiled alongside the track, where notices informed occupants of passing trains they were to be offered for sale. Of uniform size and having an even surface they were readily snapped up by jobbing builders, thousands were used to build the first section of Blackpool's Golden Mile promenade. Several discarded stone sleepers are to be seen at the bottom left-hand corner of Arthur F Tait's famous lithograph of Summit tunnel (21). The artist having placed his sketching equipment and parasol on them, and, with painstaking attention

to detail, drawn the two holes drilled on the diagonal line of each block.

21. *A F Tait's detailed lithograph of Summit tunnel*

The engineers plan to use stone block sleepers in Summit tunnel was postponed at the eleventh hour, and substituted with wooden ones. It is uncertain who was responsible for this sudden *volte-face* for both sets of drawings are signed Geo Stephenson, and countersigned Thos L Gooch. They were however used in cuttings at opposite ends of the tunnel. Which was a very odd decision to have been made in respect of the Deanroyd cutting at Lanebottom, Walsden, where the railway navvies had a particularly hard time.

DEANROYD

Ground instability at the northern end of the tunnel resulted in a complexity of engineering difficulties, problems the engineers appear to have overcome by rule of thumb decisions taken on site. Solutions chosen by the need of the moment as each impediment obstructed progress. When excavations in Deanroyd cutting revealed a large bed of natural silt, many hundreds of barrels of pitch were placed to secure a stone invert. Piles were also driven to support the side walls of the cutting. The depth of this cutting and its proximity to the Rochdale Canal proved critical when water burst into the cutting flooding the works. That calamity resulted in strengthening the intervening ground by building Deanroyd tunnel (70yd) at the point of water ingress.

The unstable ground extended towards and into the main tunnel for a short distance. To give extra support to the tunnel lining at this point a series of longitudinal wrought iron tie rods embedded in the brickwork was proposed. But the system was not adopted. Instead the last few yards of tunnel lining was executed in ashlar laid to course. The Great Oval Shaft built 60ft wide in order to secure firm footings, had effectively joined the main tunnel to its satellite at this point(22). Thus dispensing with the need of portal masonry designed and prepared to embellish the Walsden portal to something approaching the grandeur of the Summit portal. Instead the stonework was modified and used at the Summit (East) tunnel (41yd), where it now stands in splendid isolation, forming a ponderous squat looking portal to the minuscule tunnel. The final obstacle at the northern end of the tunnel was resolved by lowering Summit (East) tunnel in height, enabling a tributary of the River Calder to flow across the line of rails in a narrow conduit.

22. *Looking out through the great oval shaft and Summit East tunnel – Deanroyd cutting and tunnel beyond*

In general the use of wooden railway sleepers was restricted to that of temporary supports on new laid ground, ie. embankments. With the firm intent of replacing them with stone block sleepers after 5 to 7 years had elapsed, and the ground consolidated, events soon put paid to so illogical a plan. The wooden sleepers used on the M&L Rly. along the line and in the great tunnel, were of Larch 9ft in length with a scantling of 11in x 5in, and Kyanised to prevent decay – after John H Kyan, 1774 – 1830, inventor of a timber preservative involving total saturation in bi-carbonate of mercury. A system eventually superseded by vacuum-pressure treatment of railway sleepers with creosote oil.

In the tunnel the two innermost lines of rails were spaced 6ft 5in apart, leaving a clearance of only 3ft 8in between the outer rail and tunnel wall. At the time this was considered adequate to safeguard tunnel workers from passing trains. At a later date brick refuges were recessed into the tunnel walls, staggered at intervals of 30ft.

On the Liverpool & Manchester Rly. the ever resourceful George Stephenson had the inner-most lines of rail set at track gauge, to accommo-date extra wide loads during offpeak periods. Ingenious but highly impractical, with the entire line restricted to one direction of travel the company would have lost business.

Misalignment however minimal, at the many junctions of tunnel sections that had been worked "blind" meant that the tunnel side walls were by no means accurate enough to set the rails parallel with. Instead, at the narrowest points wooden spars were fixed across the tunnel width at a height of 6ft, from which oil-lamps were centrally suspended. Using the lighted lamps as forward sights enabled the platelayers to lay the track exactly on the tunnel mean centre line. The 2,308 lengths of rail used in Summit tunnel weighing 288.5 tons were delivered by canal barge to Lanebottom, Walsden. Each 2.5cwt rail was man-handled from the barges down into Deanroyd cutting, to be carried forward into the tunnel on flat wagons.

It was interesting, and in someways quite astonishing, to discover just how busy the canal companies were at that time. Arch-enemies they were but business was business from whatever quarter it came. Sadly for many that new found prosperity proved to be their swansong. Others soldiered on as best they could until, the age of the untethered motor lorry heralded a new door-to-door delivery service. Paradoxically the railway era came as the breath of life for Rochdale Canal. Reasoning that by owning a navigation, which for 32 miles ran almost parallel with their line, they would secure complete monopoly of all goods traffic, the M&L Rly. directors put in a bid for the Rochdale Canal during 1845. Their proposal was thwarted by some spirited opposition from the enemy of all railway companies the Aire & Calder Navigation, the Bill was lost. Even so, from 1855-90 the Rochdale was leased to a consortium of railway companies, during which time it prospered. The Midas touch culminated in fifty canal barges passing through the Summit Pass daily during the 1880s. During its tenure the canal's new management had not created a precedent, for at that time many canals were either purchased by, or leased to, various railway companies. Others were abandoned because of decreasing trade, and allowed to stagnate into unwholesome reed covered ditches.

By mid-December 1840 with 1¼ mile of double track extending into the tunnel from the Walsden portal completed, and a single line of rails only partially finished along the remaining half-mile. The work of laying the permanent way was seriously behind schedule. This disappointing reversal did nought to dampen the enthusiasm of the directors. They argued that because the brick lining had, more or less, been completed by the target date, the tunnel was to all intents and purposes deemed to be finished, so plans went ahead organising a celebration.

THE SILVER TROWEL

Wednesday 9 December 1840, dawned bright and clear, with just a slight nip in the air, the day augered well for a celebration. At Summit a multitude was reported to have gathered on the hill above the tunnel to witness the proceedings. Precisely what they had expected to see is a mystery, for the ceremony of keying in the last brick took place 200ft below them, a good half-mile inside the tunnel.

With inimitable Victorian style the event was brilliantly stage-managed with flags and buntings, plenty to eat and drink, and pieces of cannon set up on the hilltop. The official party, which included the entire engineering staff, and "Gentlemen of the first respectability", accompanied by numerous ladies, alighted from a special train in the deep cutting at Summit.

Lanterns and torches were handed to the guests

as they entered the tunnel, for without a continuous line of rails at that end of the tunnel they had perforce to walk, to where a platform had been erected between Nos 2 and 3 air shafts.

As George Stephenson, George Mould, Barnard Dickinson, and other gentlemen climbed up onto the podium at 12.00 noon precisely, the hilltop cannons were discharged, signalling the start of the ceremony. George Stephenson opened the proceedings with a short discourse addressed to Barnard Dickinson, the man chosen to perform the ceremony. In it the "Father of railways" eulogised the skillful and workmanlike manner his tunnel engineer had overcome the very peculiar difficulties encountered during the building of the tunnel. He then presented Dickinson with a silver trowel inviting him to key in the last brick, concluding his short oration with a witticism, "...I have only to add, when you key in the last brick you will be sure to take care and not waste the cement". The silver trowel was a gift from John Stephenson, the tunnel inspectors, and subcontractors. It was embellished with an engraving of the Summit tunnel portal, a crest, and inscription.

Amid prolonged and reverberated cheering and clapping Dickinson then laid the 23rd millionth brick, when order was restored he addressed the assemblage. Expressing his most sincere and hearty thanks for the very great honour bestowed upon him that day, the beautiful and munificent silver trowel, and for the cordial co-operation he had enjoyed during the building of the tunnel. He then made his now famous and strangely prophetic statement; "...The work is finished and defies the rage of tempest, fire, or war, or wasting age". The engineer's remarks foreshadowing the calamitous events of Thursday 20 December 1984, when the tunnel was engulfed by fire.

23. *Author (with camera) talking to Mr McLean of British Rail inside Summit tunnel*

After touching briefly on the subject of human suffering and the many casualties sustained during the building of the tunnel, but without specifying the actual numbers involved, Dickinson then became quite animated. Speaking in accentuated tones and gesticulating wildly the engineer continued by haranguing all and sundry, he said;

> ...The opening of this railway will no doubt occasion a great change in present channel communications: The back-bone of England may be said to be broken – its spinal marrow the Summit tunnel has been touched. Blackstone Edge! thou art no more – the grouse may still feed upon thy heather – the canal company may drain every drop of moisture from thy barren surface to sustain them in their extremity; but inns shall be deserted – thy roads will become sheep walks – no traveller will henceforth toil up thy steep side, or admire thy rugged beauty

Proprietors of certain Pennine hostelries noting with some relief that not all B. Dickinson's doom ridden prophesies actually materialised!

The ceremony at an end the party retraced its steps out of the tunnel gloom into a now sunlit deep cutting. From where they climbed a flight of extant stone steps (now disused) for the short walk along the turnpike-road to the Summit Inn. There they were invited to partake of a cold collation, during which further speeches having reference to the completion of the work were made. It was reported in the *Manchester Guardian* that, " the workmen were regaled in the tunnel". Presumably on less sumptuous fare, but with liberal supplies of liquid refreshment including on this special occasion whisky, which all railway navvies called "white beer". Travis, records that tables were set up at the bottom of the elliptical shaft at Walsden for a navvies banquet, concluding somewhat erroneously with "... after which the trains began to go through". In point of fact a further eighty-two days were to elapse before the first train carrying fare paying passengers was able to pass through the tunnel.

It was with a sense of self-satisfaction that the directors and their guests journey homeward from Summit on that December day, after all the trials and tribulations they had done it, it was finished. The first trans-Pennine railway which so many said could not be built would be fully operational in a matter of days. Those who had accused George Stephenson of "ignorance almost inconceivable in attempting so mad a project" would now have to eat their words.

There remained the small matter of those missing rails at the Summit end of the tunnel of course. But John Stephenson had eleven clear working days to sort out that trifling problem before the arrival of Sir Frederick Smith, Government Inspector of Railways on 21 December. The directors were supremely confident that, even without divine intervention, the inspector would authorise the opening of the line throughout on New Years Eve.

THE ACCIDENT

That conviction was to be very short-lived, by the following week disturbing stories were being put about, something was amiss at the tunnel, no-one seemed to know quite what, but there was talk of a collapse. Despite assurances that "the accident" was not of a serious nature the lying tongue of rumour would not be silenced. Manchester was said to be panic-stricken, leastways those Mancunians with vested interests in the new line were. Passengers arriving daily in the city by train from Littleborough brought ever more alarming tales; Yes there had indeed been a most dreadful accident, the tunnel had collapsed entombing hundreds of men – at colossal expense it would have to be opened out into a 300ft deep cutting – and worse, some said the line would have to be abandoned.

To allay the very real fears it was decided that the full M&L Rly. Board of Directors should examine the tunnel and the line beyond it, Gooch hurriedly organised yet another experimental trip. Ironically on the very day Sir Frederick Smith was to have inspected the tunnel. The directors assembled at St George's Street railway station accompanied by numerous company officials; Gill, Managing Director – Jelacorse, Secretary – Brackenbury, of the M&L solicitors Lewis & Darbyshire – Laws, Superintendant – and the upper echelon of the engineering staff, George Stephenson, Gooch, Dickinson, Mould, Young, Forsyth etc, along with the contractor John Stephenson. The private carriages used by the directors and their entourage were coupled to the front of the 9.00am scheduled train hauled by M&L Locomotive No5 *Junction* (Sharp Bros). At Littleborough station the public carriages were uncoupled and the train proceeded forward to Summit.

As the party entered the tunnel the way ahead was illuminated by fifty navvies holding lighted torches aloft. Several of the directors appeared bemused when the procession stopped at the site of "the accident" between Nos 2 & 3 air shafts.

Apart from baulks of timber spanning the tunnel walls as a precautionary measure, and pools of water standing about on the floor there was nothing to be seen, the tunnel was intact. Although being fully cognisant with the problem, and its attendant causes, George Stephenson was also viewing the accident for the first time, he said;

> ...This is a dislocated part of a very high country, where the debris has come off at a time and in a place where we could have no chance of examining it, except by excavation. But this is the only weak part we have met with

Gooch and his superior then set about explaining to the group what had happened. Hereabouts a band of blue shale passed obliquely through the workings, which when examined by the company engineers was deemed to be firm and stable. In consequence the contractor was instructed to dispense with the building of an invert in that area. On prolonged exposure to the atmosphere the blue shale had softened allowing enormous underground pressures to force the floor of the tunnel upwards and inwards, fracturing its central drainage channel. A strong torchlight was then directed upwards and George Stephenson invited everyone to examine the upper arch brickwork, which was in pristine condition. After being told that the insertion of a brick invert some 80yd in length would correct the fault – but may delay the opening by 6 to 8 weeks – the directors appeared to be perfectly satisfied with the explanations given. They then continued their inquisitorial progress through the tunnel, passing as they went along the platform where only eleven-days earlier, in happier circumstances, the last brick had been laid.

As they emerged from the tunnel into bright sunshine at Lanebottom, Walsden, the party was closely scrutinised by a gang of railway navvies peering over the parapet wall of the oval shaft. There they boarded a special train hauled by M&L Locomotive No8 *Leeds* (Shepherd & Todd) which carried them forward into the Calder Valley.

East of the Pennine watershed there was much to be seen, extensive and heavy railway engineered projects, the marvel of the age, had scarred the landscape to an alarming degree. A condition the M&L Rly. Co. endeavoured to ameliorate by planting thousands of quickthorn (hawthorn) as hedging bushes, and sowing grass seed on the embankments and cutting batters. Fortunately the Calder Valley speedily recovered its green mantle.

As the new mode of transport vied for position alongside existing means of conveyance, river, road, canal, and railway occupied the entire available space wherever the valley floor narrowed. At wider points road and rail crossed and recrossed the canal at will on splendid stone bridges and viaducts. The River Calder did not escape the onslaught, wherever it impeded progress of the all powerful locomotive machine it too was diverted from its natural course many times, including a navigable section of its lower-reaches. Only the canal stayed put, steadfastly following the valley's natural contours. Except at Walsden where the directors saw how the Rochdale Canal had been diverted into a new straight cut to avoid the expense of building two railway bridges, thus isolating a horse-shoe bend of empty waterway including, a redundant lock and its attendant lockhouse. The abandoned site, rich in sedimentary deposits, is now fortuitously occupied by Messrs Rigg's Garden Centre.

24. *Skewed railway bridge at Gauxholme, Todmorden*

The train then passed through Winterbutt Lee tunnel 306yd, on a descending gradient of 1 in 160, this tunnel had to be lined with masonry at additional cost because of soft ground. The platforms at Walsden station abut onto the northern portal of Winterbutt Lee tunnel. Opened in 1845, the station closed in 1961, and reopened as an unstaffed halt on 10 September 1990. Approaching Todmorden the line crosses the canal and Bacup Road, in fine style on the seventeen arch Gauxholme Viaduct immediately recrossing the canal on a 101ft span decorative cast-iron skew-bridge supported by four stone machicolated turrets. Architecturally the structure suffered disfigurement when necessary strengthening work was carried out in 1905. Now partially obscured from the roadway by modern low-rise flats, it is perhaps worth remembering that in its day, it was considered to be the finest example of a skewed railway bridge anywhere in the world (24).

Todmorden's first railway station, built under one of the viaduct arches remained in use until 1844, making it the longest surviving underarch ticket office on the line. That was followed by yet another temporary structure at track level until 1865, when the present station was built – 25 years after the line opened!

Todmorden was upgraded to junction status in 1849, by the opening of a scenic branch line through Cliviger Gorge (the Copy Pit Line) to Burnley. Refreshment facilities – obligatory at junction stations, were provided under contract with the adjacent Queens Hotel, a footbridge connecting the first floor of the hotel with station platforms. The town's railway architecture, dominated as it is by a splendid 54ft high nine arch viaduct which strides majestically across the town centre, was added to in 1881, when a brick wall of gargantuan proportions was raised between canal and railway. Built to secure unstable ground used as a goods yard and railway siding, it resulted in the Lancashire & Yorkshire Rly. Co. being severely criticised at the gross impropriety of building a "brick wall in stone country". Today the Great Wall of Todmorden (25) is a popular tourist attraction, listed on the town's heritage trails.

25. *The Great Wall, Todmorden*

A loud blast of the locomotive *Leeds* steam whistle, as the train reduced speed at Eastwood signalled an unscheduled stop at Charlestown. There the directors viewed the only tunnelling failure on the line. All attempts by the contractors Harding & Cropper to drive a 240yd tunnel

through a projecting hillock having failed, the project was abandoned. The set-back, caused by soft moving earth crushing completed sections of tunnel, implied no lack of competence on the part of the contractors who were awarded other M&L Rly. contracts.

The directors saw how the line had been carried round the abandoned tunnel on very tight reverse curves of 12 chains radius. In consequence of the railway diversion a "considerable diversion" of the turnpike-road had also been unavoidable. Drastic reductions in speed when approaching the Charlestown curves became second nature to all M&L Rly. engine-drivers. In 1846 work began converting the unfinished tunnel into an open cutting, along with track realignment, at which time a speed limit of 45mph was enforced. But that wasn't the end of the story.

When all the original contenders were long-dead and the memory of their epic struggle at Charlestown began to fade, fate was to play another cruel trick. On 21 June 1912, the wooded valley was the locale of a calamitous derailment involving a Manchester to Leeds express. Hauled by a L&Y Rly. 2-4-2 tank engine, four people were killed and many injured. In much happier circumstances the area is still very much on the map, as the place where the Pennine Way crosses the Calder Valley.

On through the short Weasel tunnel the special train approached Hebden Bridge, remarkable only during the 1840s because of; "A Population of 1500 souls and extensive cotton mills". And the place where many diversions of the River Calder secured a good line for the new railway. Although in Victorian times it acquired the sobriquet "Little Switzerland", today Hebden Bridge is a bustling cosmopolitan community at the heart of the South Pennine countryside.

The train sped on through Mytholmroyd where seven years later a station was built. An unusual structure with a five flight stairway, it was built partly on a viaduct, with a platform connecting pedestrian subway slung beneath one of its arches. At Luddenden Foot the pace slackened to allow a fleeting glimpse of its brand new station opened 1840 (now closed). A station with poignant memories of the gifted yet luckless Branwell Brontë (the Brontë connection with the M&L Rly. appears in Chapter 9). On through Sowerby Bridge tunnel to emerge quite suddenly into the town's first railway station, a twin turreted castellated edifice demolished after only 36-years service. The new station was sited 700yd to the east, at the junction of the aborted Sowerby Bridge – Rishworth – Smithybridge main line cut-off scheme of 1876. During the early 1980s all the station buildings were demolished, by 1985 Sowerby Bridge station was downgraded to an unstaffed halt.

FRANCIS WHISHAW

The engineer and writer Francis Whishaw considered the first series of M&L railway stations to have been too ornate. He wrote; "...Surely the engineering works will cost enough without swelling the sum total by the erection of so many "Elizabethan Villas". His rhetoric was of course that of a disillusioned man. Having been retained by the M&L as an assistant engineer – he worked alongside Gooch in preparing the estimates and parliamentary papers for the new line. All was made ready for the 1836 session of Parliament when, for some undisclosed reason Whishaw's contract was withdrawn.

26. *Crest of Manchester & Leeds Railway on the portal of Summit West tunnel. Combining the city arms of Manchester with Leeds 1839*

None of Whishaw's "Elizabethan Villas" having survived, we can but wonder whether externally the original M&L stations really were as ostentatious as he implied. Fortunately history has afforded us with a photographic peep into the past, at just one of Whishaw's "whistle-stops". An old photograph in the British Rail Collection reputedly taken in 1856 shows the first Sowerby Bridge station to have been a small multi-chimneyed structure displaying a bewildering disparity of architectural styles. Of interest are two embellishments in the form of stone shields, but what did they depict, the M&L Rly. Co. coat of arms? If so did they survive the demolition of the station in 1876? The only known sculptured example of the company coat of arms is blazoned on the portal of Summit (West) tunnel(26).

The interiors of these early stations would appear to have been the exact opposite of any undue extravagance. Using the facilities exhibited at the world's first railway station in Manchester as a yard stick, they are shown to have been Spartanly utilitarian in the extreme. Now restored and preserved in perpetuity, as part of the Castlefield Urban Heritage Park, near the city centre, George Stephenson's Liverpool Road railway station uses life-size costumed figures of passengers and railway personnel to re-create the leisurely atmosphere of a railway journey in authentic surroundings of an 1830s ticket office.

Whishaw was nought if not a freethinker, as early as the 1830s he had suggested to the M&L Rly. Co. that the erection of small shelters at intermediate stopping places would suffice. One suspects the irascible engineer would have given his wholehearted approval of the wooden platformed unstaffed halts, built along the line in recent years. Fortunately the Calder Valley Line is still graced with a few proper railway stations. Hebden Bridge was rebuilt in 1909 with ornate canopied platforms and, substantially restored to something approaching its former glory by British Rail in 1985, is a joy to behold. A place which still evokes the grandeur of the steam age.

It does seem rather odd that a workmanlike line such as the M&L should have been accused of gilding the lily with its early station-houses. Most contemporary observers consider them less grand, and not as costly as those on the adjoining North Midlands Railway. Designed by the architect Francis Thompson, who took great pride in the fact that no two NM Railway stations were alike, the free spending architects contract was understandably not renewed. Standardisation in design, with interchangeable component parts, was adopted by most railway companies for second-generation stations.

After negotiating Elland tunnel, third longest on the line, the town of Elland came into view on the right. The directors would have needed no reminding of the fact that its principle trade in 1840 was "padding and course woollen goods chiefly for the American market". Commodities destined to be carried by rail to the docks in Liverpool, but not straightaway. Although Elland railway station had opened in March 1840, through running into Liverpool did not start until 4 May 1844.

The train then entered a deep cutting at

Cromwell Bottom, the source of thousands upon thousands stone block sleepers. At a cost of 5/- each when purchased from privately owned quarries, the cutting proved to be a fortuitous bonus to the company.

At Brighouse the train traversed the splendid Rastrick Terrace and Viaduct, an enormous retaining wall and arches built in local stone. Rising almost perpendicular near the river bank, it was built to carry the line through difficult terrain of the former steeply sloped Strangstry Wood. George Stephenson never spoke a truer word when he said "...the country along the whole line abounds with the best materials for constructing a Railroad". Three-years later Robert Stephenson chose Brighouse stone when he built Victoria station in Manchester. Beyond Brighouse at Bradley Wood, in yet another deep cutting, the directors learned how fossilised trees and vast quantities of sea shells were unearthed during the excavations.

A little further down the line at Kirklees Park – the seat of Sir George Armytage, Bart, the train passed the grave of brave Robin Hood, freebooter *par excellence*, before arriving at Cooper Bridge, the station for Huddersfield. A request made to the railway company for a branch line into the town of Huddersfield which lay some 4 miles from the main line met with a discourteous reply. The M&L directors said "the town was not worth stopping a train for". Huddersfield got its railway in 1847, along with one of the finest railway stations in the country. Designed by J P Pritchett, and built in local stone with a central portico of eight enormous fluted columns, supporting a superb Palladian pediment, it originally included an hotel. Adjacent buildings also designed by Pritchett and his son formed an architectural composite greatly admired by the late Sir John Betjeman.

Next came Mirfield, which in 1841 was said to; "abound with gentlemen's seats", the town being heavily engaged in woollen manufacturing and malting. Barley and malt from "foreign parts" was delivered to the town by canal barges loaded to the gunwales, to be sprouted and dried in the many malt-kilns scattered about on the hillside. Nowadays the skyline is dominated by the green roofed towers of a monastery – The Verona Fathers.

In rather less than 2 miles they were at Thornhill Lees opposite to, and station for the ancient town of Dewsbury, once a great Christian seat of learning. The town was also world renowned as the place where the woollen blanket was invented in AD 1220. In the vicinity of Ossett the train again reduced speed to cross a wooden bridge thrown across the River Calder as a temporary measure, pending a lawsuit in Chancery. The dispute was between the M&L Rly. Co. and the proprietors of Healey Low Mills, who it was suspected were clandestinely supported by the Calder & Hebble Navigation Company. After protracted litigation the court found in favour of the railway company with costs. Work then went ahead to build a permanent crossing at a cost of £3,000.

At Horbury there was yet another of George Stephenson's underarch transitory station-houses, followed immediately by the Horbury tunnel; thirteenth and last of the planned bores, of which only twelve actually materialised. During widening work carried out in 1903 Horbury tunnel was opened out. The tunnel had emerged into an enormous rock chasm 70ft deep and three-quarters of a mile long. The prodigious Horbury cutting was the first Yorkshire contract to be taken in November 1837, and the last to be completed. The work was carried out by the contractors J B & M Flaviell.

Wakefield, erstwhile capital of the West Riding, was approached on a sixteen arch viaduct, (since filled in to form an embankment during widening work). There, the directors and their guests were to dine, but first, they journeyed on a further 3 miles to the M&L Rly. terminus at Normanton (27). What they saw, and duly inspected, was a proliferation of station buildings, goods ware-houses, and sidings all in course of erection. Built for the joint use of the Manchester & Leeds, North Midland, and York & North Midland, Railway Companies, whose lines converged at or near that point. The new station was at the hub of the early railway network, for a brief period Normanton railway station was the busiest in the north of the country, handling sixty trains a day at its peak.

Connecting trains were held for twenty minutes, allowing passengers time to use the station buffet and toilets. The comfort of its first and second-class passengers awaiting connections at Normanton was assured when, waiting-rooms, a very opulent hotel, and spacious refreshment rooms were opened in 1842. Under the management of Francis Josey, late of the Palatine Club, Liverpool, Normanton railway hotel became the model for many railway hotels throughout the land. Built as an integral part of the station it afforded private access to the railway platforms.

A novel feature built for the convenience and safety of all passengers was a glass covered pedestrian footbridge over the lines of rails. One of the first to be constructed.

27. *End of the original M&L Rly. line —
A F Tait's view of Normanton railway
station and hotel*

At 2pm the directors and their guests returned to Wakefield alighting at the station in Kirkgate, from where they hastened to the George Inn for a hearty meal. Henry Holdsworth Esq. presided at the repast, and from the chair announced that because the days proceedings were running late there would be but one toast. He gave, "...Success to the Manchester & Leeds Railway", which was loudly applauded. Of all the wonderous things they had seen in the Calder Valley that day, the problems at Summit tunnel remained uppermost in the minds of all the directors. After the meal, in the quiet of the George Inn saloon they put some very searching questions to George Stephenson relating to the recent accident. He replied by reiterating much of what had been said earlier in the day, but reassured everyone with his now famous pronouncement;

> ..."I will stake my character, my head, if that tunnel can give way to bring danger to any public passing through", ending his speech on a triumphant note with – "...It is the greatest work that has yet been done of this kind, taking it as a whole I don't think there is such another piece of work in existence in the world".

A consensus of opinions amongst the directors appears to have been that the time factor in delaying the opening of the tunnel was a bitter disappointment. But the cost of carrying out the necessary remedial work was judged to be negligible. Indeed, when told that the repair bill would be in the region of £3,000 – 4,000 Henry Holdsworth declared, "...it must be considered a mere bagatelle in a work of this kind".

The party then wended its way back to the railway station for the return trip, at the entrance to Summit tunnel they separated. Some of the more energetic gentlemen opted to walk over the top road through Dog Isles, Calderbrook village, before dropping down to Summit. The majority retracing their perambulation through the tunnel to an awaiting train in the deep cutting. Despite being the shortest day of the year it had remained bright and sunny throughout. It also marked the last official duty George Stephenson performed as Engineer-in-Chief to the M&L Rly. Co. The seriousness of the tunnel invert failure delaying the opening of the line throughout marred his departure. And in all probability, dissuaded the engineer from delivering a valediction to the assembled directorate. Ten-days later he resigned, and Thomas Longridge Gooch, appointed a worthy successor.

9. TUNNEL TAILPIECE

Sir Frederick Smith's report had not of course included the stricken tunnel, although he did examine the short section of line between it and Littleborough station, along with 7 miles of track between Hebden Bridge and the northern portal of Summit tunnel. Both were found to have been solidly constructed, the government inspector sanctioned the opening of both sections for public transport on 4 January 1841. Messrs Lacey & Allen's horse-drawn omnibuses then carried rail passengers the much shorter distance between Littleborough station and Lanebottom, Walsden. Where they entrained in the Deanroyd cutting.

THE PHANTOM RAILWAY STATION

Recent speculation that Littleborough may have had a second railway station sited nearer to Summit tunnel would appear to be somewhat at variance with the records.

At a meeting held in Manchester during February 1839, George Stephenson and Thomas L Gooch were joined by Robert Stephenson, George's son, who it was reported rendered invaluable assistance in the design, layout, and siting of railway stations at Manchester, Rochdale, and Littleborough. Contrary to a fictionalised version of events at Summit tunnel as portrayed in the novel *World From Rough Stones* by Malcolm Macdonald. This was Robert Stephenson's only direct involvement with the construction of the M&L Rly. prior to 1844 when he built the lines new western terminus Victoria station, Manchester.

The following abstract from an engineers report of that meeting in Manchester, would suggest that a second Littleborough station may have been contemplated at one time.
> ...The line will be finished to within 180yd of the tunnel by May next year: but as there is no suitable place for a station there, It will not be desirable to open it further than Littleborough

11 March 1839

signed Geo Stephenson
Thomas L Gooch

One theory, purely speculative, is that the idea of a second railway station might have resulted from an announcement made on 2 March 1840. Clearly touting for business the notice informed the general public that, "The stations for the reception of goods at Manchester and Littleborough are now ready for the carriers". With the arrival and departure of goods trains at Littleborough, congestion in the narrow streets adjacent to the station would have been considerable. The notion that in order to alleviate this pressure, through passengers were carried forward a short distance beyond the station into open country. Where they would alight onto temporary platforms, and then walk across flat fields to board awaiting horse-drawn omnibuses on the turnpike-road, would appear to fit very neatly into that scenario. Too neatly in fact for it would have been illegal.

It has been noted that Sir Frederick Smith did not sanction the opening of the line between Littleborough station and Summit tunnel until 4 January 1841. Only eight-weeks before the tunnel opened on 1 March, hardly worth the trouble and expense of making alternative arrangements for so short a period. The foregoing facts would suggest the existence, however transitory, of Littleborough's metaphoric second railway station – for that is what temporary wooden platforms built in the middle of nowhere would have amounted to, requires considerably more research and clarification.

———————————

After his inspection Sir Frederick journeyed north into Scotland to examine other railway projects. Upon his return to Summit in February of the following year, the tunnel repairs had been completed just as Gooch and his former chief said they would be. The government inspector had no hesitation in pronouncing the tunnel safe, and authorised its opening to public transport on Monday 1 March 1841. The first train to pass through was symbolically a goods train hauled by M&L Locomotive No 30 *Manchester* (Sharp, Roberts & Co), closely followed by the 7.00am passenger service out of Manchester. For a time the passenger service was restricted to ten trains on weekdays, and four on Sundays. By 1856 the service had improved only slightly, to thirteen trains into Manchester and ten to Leeds.

With the line now fully operational celebrations to mark its completion were low-key and informal. A convenient time-lapse between the third and fourth scheduled trains on the down-line, allowed the directors freedom of the rails between Manchester and Wakefield. Their special train included the two hybrid coaches *Gondola* and *Tourist* suitably bedecked with bunting. It travelled at speed stopping only to pick up one band of musicians at Summit tunnel, and another at Ossett.

Luncheon was served in a goods warehouse at Wakefield railway station, the town entering into the spirit of the occasion when all the church bells were rung "right merrily". The guest of honour at the repast was the new M&L Rly. Engineer-in-Chief, Thomas Longridge Gooch. As a token of their esteem, and in recognition of his service as resident engineer during the construction of the line, the directors presented Gooch with a gift of £1,000. From the engineering staff he received a testimonial in the form of an illuminated address, and a tea service. George Stephenson, invited as an honoured guest was content to take a passive role in the proceedings, and did not speak at the luncheon.

For a short time Summit tunnel had the distinction of being the longest operational railway tunnel in the world, but was superseded when, on 30 June 1841 Brunel opened his famous Box tunnel 3,212yd, on the Great Western Railway. Summit's claim to world fame had lasted just four-months, but all was not lost. For 75 years Summit tunnel remained the longest of 92 tunnels owned and operated by the Lancashire & Yorkshire Rly. Co. and still ranks fifteenth longest in Britain.

To facilitate safe transit through the newly opened Summit tunnel a pneumatic telegraph was installed. Compressed air was used to operate audible signals at both ends of the tunnel, A F Tait depicted the Summit signal cabin in his famous lithograph (21). This was a curious decision to have taken for the electric telegraph, patented in 1837, was first put to practical use on the railways. In a speech made at Blackburn, Lancashire, in December 1840, George Stephenson spoke enthusiastically of an electric telegraph he had witnessed in operation on the London – Blackwall line. Where it was ineptly referred to as "a railway talking machine".

In his book *The Lancashire & Yorkshire Railway*, 1896, Thomas Normington, records that an electric telegraph was installed at Summit tunnel in 1859. He relates how the telegraphist gave notice to his fellow operator whenever a train was about to enter the tunnel with "a tick on the telegraph needle", which was always acknowledged. No other train being permitted to enter the tunnel on the same line of rails until a safe transit signal had been received.

Although this was a decided improvement on the antiquated pneumatic telegraph, the single-needle electric telegraph was flawed by its inability to hold and display messages. The

instant an operator took his finger off the telegraph key the message was cancelled. When such messages as; "is tunnel clear" – "tunnel clear" – "tunnel blocked", had to be committed to memory by the receiving telegraphist. A rapid succession of like messages transmitted in times of peril, would often leave the operator confused as to the order in which they had been received. Consequently, the very man whose job it was to prevent tunnel collisions actually caused them.

Normington, also mentions some form of block telegraph being installed at all long tunnels on the line in 1865. If true this was a tardy response by the company to a Board of Trade directive on tunnel safety circulated to every railway company in the land. The directive was issued after an appalling accident in Clayton tunnel on the London & South Coast Railway in 1861. But it is, of course, well-documented that it was in 1873, the direct result of a government imposed safety campaign that block signalling was adopted at high cost along the entire line, starting at Summit tunnel. Today the tunnel is controlled by Preston power signal box.

In his authoritative three-volumed work *The Lancashire & Yorkshire Railway*, John Marshall, warns that Normington should be read with caution.

Thomas Normington 1824 – 1916

He began his 40 year career with the L&Y Rly. Co. as a parcels porter at Brighouse station where diligence, plus a propensity for hard work, earmarked him for rapid promotion. Progressing through the ranks he was appointed station-master at Mumps station, Oldham. In his book he recounts some hair-raising anecdotes about the Oldham – Werneth 1 in 27 rope operated incline. On the occasion of a royal visit to Halifax in August 1863, when the Prince of Wales opened the new Town Hall, Normington was appointed co-ordinator responsible for the movement of 114 trains carrying 125,000 passengers into and out of Halifax railway station during a nine hour period; a task he carried out with aplomb. He retired as Eastern District Superintendent at Wakefield in 1895. Believing his pension entitlement to be lower than that paid to other company officials of equal rank, he carried out a war of attrition against the company.
Unfortunately his behaviour marred his book of the following year, in it he castig-

ates the Board of Directors almost to the point of absurdity. Perhaps the way the book was penned also contributed to its many errors, especially with dates. Apparently Normington dictated the entire work from memory to his long-suffering wife who copied it out in longhand. In spite of its misgivings the book has some merit, after all the man was there during the company's formative years, and, as Marshall points out it certainly makes entertaining reading.

In 1916 while the rest of humanity was locked in mortal conflict, Thomas Normington died, still fighting his own war against the L&Y Rly. Co. Sadly he died an embittered old man.

The advent of rail travel created many problems for the promoters of railways, none more so than with tunnels, the public at large were terrified of the dark cavernous holes. Aversions that were exacerbated by the rantings of some hell-fire preachers who, seized on the analogy that the man-made bores, and Lucifer's satanic underworld, were one and the same. A form of sanctimonious hypocrisy the railway promoters could have done without. Nor was public antipathy allayed by opinions expressed in the medical profession. Which predicted a dire catastrophe to the minds and bodies of all those unfortunate wretches who passed through the hell-holes. A Dr. Chalmers of Liverpool poured oil on troubled waters when he assured potential passengers. Even speeds of 34mph would cause no inconvenience or alarm, nor would the eye be disturbed while "viewing the scenery".

One man who did view the diverse scenery of Lancashire during the first half of the nineteenth century was the northern writer Edwin Butterworth 1812 – 1848. Born in Oldham the son of the town Postmaster, he is perhaps best remembered as the young man who carried out the onerous task of visiting every parish and township in the County Palatine on foot, collecting and recording the historical data Edward Baines used in his *History of Lancashire*, published in 1836.

Butterworth, published two works on the M&L Rly. the first dated 1839, *An Historical Sketch of the Manchester & Leeds Railway as far as completed*, would appear to be lost. The Lancashire Bibliography indicated two copies of the work at Wigan and Oldham Public Libraries respectively, both have failed to trace the 28 page booklet. The other work: *Views on the*

Manchester and Leeds Railway, drawn from Nature on Stone by A F Tait, with a Descriptive History by Edwin Butterworth, published in folio 1845, and since reissued, is a railway classic.

We are indebted to Edwin Butterworth for his descriptive prose, in particular the marvellous account of a journey he made through Summit tunnel during the early 1840s. As a piece of railway tunnel narrative it has never been bettered.

> ...The rapidity of the flight, the screech of the warning signal from the engine, the overhanging column of mingled smoke and steam, the rush of air, together with the lurid glare and innumerable sparks thrown by the flambeaux which the train carries and others borne by persons stationed in the tunnel conspire with feeling that we are passing through the body of a huge mountain, to excite and awe the mind; for there we are, if out or peril, yet, in the very midst of the highest triumphs of human enterprise.

To appease the very real fears of its claustrophobic first customers the M&L Rly. Co. had attempted to transform the tunnel into a lighted gallery by torchlight, during each four-minute transit of a passenger train. Such absurdities quickly faded away as the travelling public realised that to journey through a subterranean passage was only like "passing in a coach by night along a narrow street".

Edwin Butterworth had obviously been seated in an enclosed carriage. Had he been travelling third-class he would have been made painfully aware that some of the sparks were in fact red-hot cinders, emitted by the locomotive's powerful steam blast. Burning embers ricocheting off the tunnel roof rained down on the helpless Stanhopers, singeing hair, and burning holes in their shabby clothing. Clearly the high quality coke purchased at a bargain price of only 14s per ton from Low Moor, nr Bradford, which it was said "did not clinker on the fire bars", also provided a fiery pyrotechnic display. While travelling towards Manchester, Thomas Normington discovered on emerging from Summit tunnel a large hole burned in his top hat! One can but wonder why Normington, an up-and-coming M&L official was travelling in an open Stanhope carriage in the first place. But then this trans-Pennine railway was not without its fair share of oddities. Nobody has yet satisfactorily explained why so many of its early officials and company servants were blessed with shocks of carrot red hair.

When Gladstone's Railway Regulations Act of 1844 became law, it effectively transformed and humanised rail travel, from the rough-and-tumble of the early years to something approaching the order of today. Thereafter every railway company was required by law to convey its third-class passengers at a rate of; not exceeding one penny per mile, at a speed of not less than 12mph, and in carriages fitted with seats and roofs. The Act further required and compelled each and every company, to run one such train daily in both directions stopping at every station on the line. The M&L Rly. Co. already conformed to the latter requirement, it had been running mixed class trains daily, four on Sundays, in both directions since 1841. The minimum speed regulation was introduced to circumvent certain less reputable companies who attached third-class carriages to slow moving goods trains. Also, those thoroughly despicable operators, who whitewashed the insides of goods wagons and used them on excursion specials. After Gladstone's timely intervention trains catering for all classes of rail travel were dubbed "Parliamentary Trains" by the railway companies, and epitomised "Parlys" by an ever grateful proletariat. The great Parliamentarian often travelled third-class, to ensure his reforms were being enacted.

Conditions for third-class passengers remained Spartan, seats were of slotted wooden bench construction shorn of upholstery, many without back-rests. But with every class of passenger now protected from the elements and safe from physical hurt, the fear of tunnels slowly began to recede. The dread of underground conveyance was followed by a reticent acceptance of the fact that all rail tunnels were unavoidable necessities. By the turn of the century the travelling public at large, joyously liberated from its fears of hell-holes, satanic underworlds, and such like aberrations, poked fun at tunnels, using them to highlight the chastened humour of that bygone age. For most passengers young and old alike, the anticipated thrill of approaching and passing through a long railway tunnel at speed remained an exhilarating experience – it still does.

SUMMIT EXODUS

Events at Summit had brought together a remarkable group of talented people, each quite exceptional in his own sphere, and now it was time to go their separate ways. The most famous name was of course George Stephenson, whose immortality was assured long before Summit, not because of it. Although he had surveyed the lines route through the Summit Pass twice, the daily minutia of building its great tunnel he very sensibly entrusted to others. The real *tour de force* at Summit was unquestionably the work of John Stephenson. Although many another contractor of repute could and would have built the tunnel, he it was who unravelled the sorry plight Copeland & Evans got themselves into. Using considerable administrative skill and an immodest haste, he had achieved a firm completion date set by the Board with comparative ease, albeit at fearful cost in human suffering.

28. *Summit tunnel c1925, Lancashire & Yorkshire Rly. platelayers proudly displaying the tools of their trade, including two primitive oil lamps*

Under the terms of his contract John Stephenson was required to maintain the tunnel fabric, and its permanent way, for a period of twelve calendar months after completion. To meet that requirement he left a skeleton staff behind at Summit. Others who stayed were selected workers enlisted to form the nucleus of the M&L Rly. Police Force. The directors in their wisdom reasoned that, by recruiting only those who had laboured to build the line they would guard it more assiduously than outsiders. One week after final completion of the tunnel John Stephenson received a summary of accounts and final payment, but had to wait a further three months for the £10,000 bond held as surety by the company. This was because the tunnel accident had delayed the opening, even though the contractor had been exonerated from all blame, the Board withheld repayment until the tunnel became fully operational.

George Stephenson 1781 – 1848

Towards the close of a busy life the "Father of Railways" withdrew from the public eye enjoying the lifestyle of a prosperous country gentleman at Tapton House. The engineer's second wife Elizabeth having died in 1845, his housekeeper Ellen Gregory, a farmer's daughter from Bakewell, Derbyshire, became the third Mrs Stephenson, just six-months prior to his own demise from fever on 12 August. He died an unbeliever worshipping a lesser god – the Locomotive. He once told Robert Summerside, a lifelong colleague, "...I am a better Christian than many of those priests. Ah! Summerside, I will send the locomotive as the great Missionary over the world" – and he did. Religious feelings apart, in the materialistic age in which he lived the railway, which he founded and perfected, but did not invent, probably did more good for the whole of mankind than any other single invention of that century.

On the day of the great engineer's funeral newspapers appeared with heavy black mourning-borders. Civic dignitaries and workmen followed the cortège from Tapton House to Trinity Church, Chesterfield, where he was laid to rest. And – Edward Pease, the 81-year-old Quaker, and lifelong friend, was the only man to keep his hat on throughout the burial service.

Obituary Notice in the
Derby & Chesterfield Reporter
18 August 1848
What faults he had (and who will pretend that he was without them) cease to be remembered, now he is no more. Take him for all in all we shall not look upon his like again.

Thomas Longridge Gooch
1808 – 1882 MICE 1845

For three-years after the opening of the line the engineer-in-chief was engaged in the winding-up of heavy main line contracts, and laying out its many branch lines, principally those into Heywood, Oldham and Halifax. In 1844 Gooch resigned from the M&L Rly. Co. to be succeeded by Mr, later Sir, John Hawksworth. His services much sought after during the Railway Mania Gooch worked harder than ever until, at the age of forty-two he broke down in health, and was compelled to retire. The remainder of his life being devoted to charitable work, attending to the welfare of soldiers on overseas stations.

John Stephenson 1794 – 1848

After Summit the railway contractor assumed control of the extraordinarily difficult Chorley tunnel and cutting, which was followed by other work on the Bolton & Preston Rly. and the Blackburn – Preston line. While on a visit to the North Midland Rly. at Rotherham on 8 July 1848, in connection with a maintenance contract for that line, John Stephenson collapsed and died aged fifty-four. The builder of Summit tunnel was buried at the General Cemetery, Rotherham, South Yorkshire.

Barnard Dickinson

The resident engineer at Summit tunnel may be truly described as the will-o-the-wisp member of the Summit team, for research has revealed nothing of his antecedence or subsequent career. The recipient of much adulation and goodwill, he walked away from Summit clutching his silver trowel, and disappeared into oblivion. In 1846 a Barnard Dickinson Jnr. was appointed engineer to the East Lancashire Rly. Co. – the Summit tunnel engineer's son?

George Mould

As one of the old guard of valiant railwaymen – he was a contemporary of Woodhouse, Jee, Errington, Dodds etc, the greats of early railway history. Mould was in all probability the oldest member of the Summit team. He remained with the firm Stephenson, McKenzie & Brassey, and was still at work in its Glasgow office during 1847.

John Curphey Forsyth
1815 – 1879 MICE 1853

After assisting with the parliamentary plans, Forsyth prepared most of the contract drawings for the new line, including some of the voluminous Summit tunnel drawings, at the Manchester drawing office. Afterwards he was promoted resident engineer of a 7 – 8 mile section of the main line near Huddersfield. During 1843-4 he worked on the building of Victoria station, Manchester, he died at Newcastle-upon-Tyne in poor health.

Copeland & Evans

In spite of James Copeland's obvious eccentricities one cannot but admire the tunnel mavericks tenacity in taking on the Shildon tunnel contract. Particularly after the Summit tunnel debacle landed him in prison as an improvident debtor. He was in all probability incarcerated at Lancaster Castle, which until 1869 served as a debtors prison for the entire county. John Evans fared rather better when operating as an independent contractor, as witnessed by his construction work for the M&L Rly. Co. at Bolton and Darwen in 1839 and 1845 respectively.

ANTHONY HARDING

During 1817 Harding was employed at the Bobby Colliery, West Moor, on Tyneside, piling coal into heaps by horse-drawn sled. A mode of working rendered redundant when George Stephenson laid out a network of tramway lines at the pit. It is to be presumed the stripling came under the influence of the great engineer about that time. He next appeared as a fully trained subengineer and thirteen-years later was working as a section engineer at Edgehill tunnel in Liverpool. Duties Harding carried out with some distinction, he was rewarded by being elected to drive the locomotive *Meteor* hauling one of eight trains used in procession at the grand opening of the Liverpool & Manchester Rly. in 1830. At Summit tunnel Harding was subordinate to the resident engineer Dickinson, where he does not appear to have been singled out for any special mention. Indeed, but for Whishaw's one-line reference to "another engineer at the tunnel named Mr. Harding", we may never have known of his involvement.

DR. BARKER

In addition to his appointment as surgeon to the Summit Tunnel Sickness & Burial Benefit Society, and a successful practice in Littleborough, John Barker MD had married well. His wife Mary née Mills (or Milne) had financial interests in coalmines at Shaw, near Oldham. Sadly the prosperous doctor dissipated his assets on the demon drink and died young.

JAMES WALKER
1781 – 1862 MICE 1823

Although this engineers involvement with the M&L Rly. Co. was minimal, and with the Summit tunnel nonexistent, it should be remembered that the route he proposed from the Calder Valley through Wyke and Low Moor was, more or less, subsequently adopted. Being a far superior line to George Stephenson's meander to Normanton, it is still used today. Walker, a Scotsman born and bred, died in Edinburgh.

TUNNEL TALES

FROM FOUL TO FAIR

During its first winter M&L Rly. passengers observed that on entering the tunnel at Summit in dense fog, a train invariably emerged into bright sunshine at Walsden. A climatic phenomenon that had previously gone unnoticed before the railway era. The reason was, of course, both geological and climatic, heavy glacial clay deposits west of the Pennines were a major contributory factor to rising vapours which

caused the fog. Whereas the Calder Valley being predominantly absorbent millstone-grit had the opposite effect. It also explained the poor scheduling of trains into and out of Manchester during the winter months of last century.

U. *Percival Skelton's highly inaccurate woodcut engraving of Summit in the 1840s*

EMPTY CARRIAGES

With most trains bereft of passengers at the Pennine Divide the Summit tunnel became a barometer, indicating the social habits of people in both counties during the mid-Victorian era. Few could afford the fare, or for that matter had the need, to travel to Manchester or Leeds – save the well-to-do millowners and exporters. Instead the populace at large used the railway for short journeys, much the same as succeeding generations used electric trams, one mode of public transport that did not penetrate the Summit Pass. The Halifax tramway system got as far as Hebden Bridge, and in August 1905, Rochdale trams terminated at the Summit Inn, leaving a 9 mile gap unserviced. This was because Todmorden never operated an electric tramway system, but took the unprecedented step from horse-drawn to motor omnibuses. In consequence of this the lifestyles of those living at or near the county boundaries remained well-defined, long after a main line railway thundered beneath their feet. Even today people living at opposite ends of Summit tunnel speak the vestiges of noticeably different dialects.

ANTHONY GRAY (DECEASED)

A collision in Summit tunnel on Wednesday 21 June 1843, was reported in the *Bradford Observer*. Apparently engine-driver Gray was taking a train of empty carriages through when he ran into the rear of a goods train on the curves at the Walsden end of the tunnel. Damage to rolling-stock was minimal and there were no injuries. On the following Sunday Gray was driving a luggage-train from Manchester to Brighouse. At 3pm while passing Clegg Hall, between Rochdale and Littleborough, the drawbar connecting the engine to its tender suddenly snapped causing the engine to surge forward. Gray was thrown backwards off the footplate onto the line, where he was struck by the following wagons, severing his head and both legs. A direct result of this appalling accident, the first reported failure of the two-inch diameter drawbar, was all M&L Rly. engines and tenders being fitted with side chains, additional to the drawbar.

JUST PASSING THROUGH

After undergoing a major overhaul at the Hunslet Engine Works in Leeds during 1969, the privately owned former LNER Locomotive No 4472 *Flying Scotsman* passed through Summit tunnel en route to Liverpool, from where it was shipped to America for an extended tour.

WARS OF THE ROSES

One lasting outcome of that protracted and disastrous dynastic struggle between the Houses of York and Lancaster, was a friendly rivalry existing between the two counties. Each affirming its supposed superiority over the other at cricket, and other mundane pursuits. It was all very much tongue-in-cheek of course, for when the railway age interposed a tunnel between the Historic Shires, that too became the butt of much good-humoured intercounty raillery. It was said by many a music-hall comic, that each and every £1 passing through Summit tunnel into Yorkshire would cost the Lancastrians 30/- to repossess.

THE BRONTË CONNECTION

Like most Victorians all members of the Brontë household, save perhaps prim Aunt Branwell, took to the new railways as ducks to water. The distaff side being the most travelled, with Charlotte top of the rail mileage league. Because of her frequent visits to Mrs Gaskell in Didsbury, Manchester, she also made most passes through Summit tunnel. All the surviving Brontë girls: Charlotte, Emily, and Ann, invested their Aunt Branwell legacies in the Midland Rly. Co. But, acting against Charlotte's advice to sell – sell lost heavily when the George Hudson "Empire" collapsed.

The family used Keighley railway station, some 4 miles from Haworth Parsonage, a distance occasionally covered in the station fly or by the village two-wheeled gig, but most often they walked, both ways. It was this hindrance that prompted the Revd. Patrick Brontë to chair a committee which carried out a feasibility study into building a railway between Haworth and Hebden Bridge, a forlorn venture defeated by the hilly terrain. The Revd. Brontë's most traumatic train journey was through Summit tunnel, and on to Manchester, where the aging cleric underwent a cataract operation. In happier vein he visited the capital by rail.

In July 1840 Branwell Brontë, applied to Captain Laws RN for the position of Assistant Clerk-in-Charge at Sowerby Bridge station. The application which proved successful carried a salary of £75 per annum commencing in October. His work at Sowerby Bridge must have been entirely satisfactory, the following April he was promoted to Clerk-in-Charge (Station-Master) at Ludden-den Foot, at a starting salary of £130. At first all went well but the enigmatic Branwell soon tired of the humdrum existence, he yearned for the fleshpots which thus far had eluded him. To remedy that omission he got into the habit of leaving a porter in charge of the booking-office, while he imbibed at the Lord Nelson Inn, in Luddenden. A hostelry still open 150 years after the wayward Branwell's sad demise.

When the station accounts were submitted for audit in April 1842 a deficit of £11 1s 7d was discovered. Unable to account for the missing money Branwell Brontë was summarily dismissed, and the shortfall deducted from his salary. He was, of course, no thief, but had been guilty of gross negligence. A porter named Walton had been helping himself to the takings while the station-master drank.

On the 11 April a signed memorial from some wealthy millowners, merchants, and the local gentry, was sent up the line to the M&L Rly. Co. head office in Manchester. It respectfully requested the directors to reinstate Mr Brontë as Clerk-in-Charge at Luddenden Foot railway station forthwith. The Board after due consideration decided to uphold the notice of dismissal. Branwell Brontë returned home to Haworth Parsonage in disgrace.

Tunnel Diary

6 September 1837
Contract to build Summit tunnel signed by Copeland & Evans

17 August 1838
First brick laid at bottom of No 10 air shaft

18 March 1839
Second tunnel contract signed by John Stephenson

31 May 1839
Experimental trip to Summit tunnel by directors of M&L Rly. Co. to inspect progress

3 July 1839
Opening ceremony of M&L Rly. line to Littleborough, guests also visited Summit tunnel

10 December 1839
While making an experimental trip to Summit tunnel, a train travelling at 30mph crashed at Rochdale

21 December 1840
Experimental trip to inspect the accident that delayed the opening of Summit tunnel

1 March 1841
Summit tunnel officially opened to public transport. It had cost £251,000 and 41 lives

21 June 1843
Collision in Summit tunnel; wagons damaged but no injuries

20 September 1884
The 1.25pm passenger train from Leeds – Liverpool while travelling at speed derailed in Summit tunnel. 10 passengers shaken

29 August 1899
Manchester express broke down in Summit tunnel

11 September 1901
Heavy flooding blocked Summit tunnel

6 February 1922
Passenger train ran into goods train in Summit tunnel – no injuries

20 December 1984
Petrol tanker train derailed in Summit tunnel burst into flames

17 August 1985
Todmorden Round Table organised charity walk through Summit tunnel 5,500 people attended

19 August 1985
Summit tunnel reopened to public transport after extensive repairs costing £1 million

1 March 1991
Summit tunnel 150th anniversary

A Phoenix-Like Paragon

Almost 144 years after it first opened to traffic Summit tunnel achieved worldwide notoriety when television pictures of its sensational fire – the worst tunnel fire in British railway history – were beamed around the world by satellite. The writer, visiting New Zealand a few days after the fire, was inundated with questions about the accident by expatriate northerners, who had seen and recognised the tunnel on New Zealand television.

The drama began when a train of thirteen bulk tankers owned by Procor (UK) Ltd, carrying 780 tonnes of four star petrol from Haverton Hill, Middlesbrough, Cleveland, to an I.C.I. chemical plant at Glazebrook, near Warrington, Cheshire, entered Summit tunnel just before 6.00am on Thursday 20 December 1984.

A little beyond half-a-mile into the tunnel, the failure of a reconditioned roller bearing axle-box on the fourth tanker caused a derailment, which in turn severed its automatic breaking system, bringing the train to a shuddering standstill, it was 5.50am precisely.

The train crew, Stanley Marshall, driver, aged 50yrs of Eccles, and Graham Broadbent, guard, aged 25yrs, of Rawtenstall, along with Stanley Smalley, a guard inspector, who was hitching a lift home. They all jumped down from the footplate into the darkness, the locomotives lights were still functioning but shining forward. As they peered along the train flames could be seen, but they appeared to be on the opposite track. What they saw was the seventh tanker toppled over on its side blocking the down-line and burning fiercely. A strong smell of smoke and fumes followed by a "sudden whoosh noise" (sic), alerted Marshall to the possibility of an imminent explosion, he said "...let's get out of here" as they fled the tunnel. First out after the 1 mile dash to Summit was the youngest and fittest man Broadbent. He raised the alarm by telephoning Preston power signal-box, they in turn rang Smithybridge signal-box where detonators were placed on the rails, and signals set at danger. Presumably similar precautions were taken at the Yorkshire end of the tunnel.

Intercounty emergency services – Police, Fire, and Ambulance crews from Greater Manchester, Lancashire, and Calderdale, Yorkshire, arrived quickly and set up headquarters at their respective ends of the tunnel. For a time, communications were a problem due to the height of surrounding hills. But improved significantly when a 90ft high hydraulic platform carrying an improvised aerial was positioned on the top road above the tunnel, enabling the mobile command centre to relay messages to all units.

At the request of Greater Manchester firemen the train driver, and both guards, re-entered the tunnel at Summit to retrieve the locomotive and three undamaged tankers. A task they performed with great courage, not made any easier by the metal couplings having become too hot to handle.

29. *Summit tunnel at the height of the conflagration*

At 7.00am firemen from various Calderdale units entered the tunnel at Walsden, to start what proved to be a three-and-a-half-hour battle. They were accompanied by Brian Dinsdale, a British Rail maintenance engineer, and Donald Stott, a section supervisor, resident in Summit Village. Approaching the train from the rear they made tankers safe, and successfully dealt with numerous small fires in the tunnel ballast, caused by leaking petrol, extinguishing them with foam. But as the firefighters, now wearing breathing apparatus, set to work on the toppled seventh tanker the intense heat blew its safety vents. Moments later the tanker exploded;

fortunately the resultant fire-ball shot up an air shaft and no-one was injured. Station Officer Ralph Mallinson, of Halifax, West Yorkshire, decided he could no longer risk the lives of his men as the situation had now become a fire-bomb, he gave the emergency signal to evacuate the tunnel. Scarcely six-minutes after the smoke blackened exhausted firemen emerged from the tunnel, ominous rumblings deep inside the hill could be heard. The smoke billowing from an air shaft suddenly darkened, moments later an enormous explosion shook the hillside as another tanker exploded. Once again the fire-ball shot up the ventilation shaft, rising to a height of 150 metres – a truly awesome sight (29).

That was the signal to implement a contingency plan involving the evacuation of upwards of 200 people residing and working near the tunnel entrances. The real possibility that the next fire-ball might bypass the air shafts causing a blowback along the tunnel cavity with catastrophic effect, could no longer be ignored. Fleets of ambulances and police cars carried the young, old, and infirm to places of safety, some were worried about having to leave pets behind.

Despite the combined efforts of 200 intrepid firefighters using the most up-to-date equipment the fire raged on out of control. It peaked at midday when flames appeared from a second air shaft for a time, and took three-days to burn itself out.

Not all the petrol ignited in this bizzare fire, of the ten tankers involved the last two although severely damaged survived the conflagration with a quantity of petrol inside them. From the remaining eight tankers 40,000 gallons spilled out as the tankers split open in the intense heat, most, but not quite all to be consumed by fire. Some 5 miles away in Rochdale, the River Roch carried a pervasive smell of petrol through the town centre.

At 11.00am two teams of firemen using specialist equipment began pumping high expansion foam down the two air shafts immediately adjacent to the seat of the fire. This proved to be a masterstroke, albeit an expensive one, for it effectively prevented the danger of a blowback along the tunnel, and, by starving the flames of air substantially reduced the intensity of the blaze. Eight-days later British Rail engineers were able to carry out the first tentative examination of the fire ravaged tunnel.

What they saw was a scene of utter devastation, almost a quarter-mile of track had been buckled by derailment and fire, the floor of the tunnel lay littered with brick-dust. Of the eight tankers destroyed some were seen to have been torn apart by explosion, while others having imploded lay limp and deflated like squashed sausages. Bogeys and wheels had been torn off and thrown against the tunnel wall with considerable force. At points in the tunnel where six courses of brickwork had been laid the outer course had perished in the inferno and fallen away, leaving the second course severely damaged but still in place. Temperatures in excess of 1,500°C had caused brickwork at the periphery of the fire to melt and run down the walls "like treacle" (30).

30. *Molten brickwork ran down the walls "like treacle"*

Emerging from the tunnel after the two hour inspection John Searson, of British Rail, said "...The overriding impression in there is how lucky we are that the structure has not been irreparably damaged". That first official comment went someway to repudiate a rumour, rife in the tabloid press, that British Rail might use the tunnel fire as a convenient excuse to close the line. In the event BRs commitment to its Calder Valley line was total; before the fire revenue had actually been increasing, after it, they had plans for George Stephenson's line of easy gradients.

Before lighting could be installed, along with heavy lifting gear, the stricken tunnel had first to be made safe. A team of experts from Imperial Chemical Industries removed several pockets of fuel over a three-day period in early January, including 2,000 gallons of petrol pumped out of the two tankers at the end of the train. Work then started to remove all ten tankers and other debris, a protracted operation hampered by the

confined space and damaged track. The last piece of wreckage was removed from the tunnel on 4 March, to be taken to a scrap-metal yard in Rotherham, South Yorkshire (31). The detached roller bearing axle-box which had caused the accident, was recovered from underneath the tenth tanker with the broken axle end inside it. It was sent away to British Rail Research & Development Centre at Derby for detailed examination.

31. *Last of the wrecked tankers en route to the scrap-metal yard in Rotherham, South Yorkshire*

A Department of Transport inquiry into the accident was held at the Portland Thistle Hotel, Manchester, on 8 February, by Mr D A Sawyer, Inspecting Officer of Railways. It was revealed that the Summit tunnel track had been sound, having only recently been relaid ultrasonic tests were carried out just four-days before the accident. The findings of the inquiry was that axle failure had caused the derailment "by a cause yet to be determined".

By now speculation in daily newspapers had switched from "If" to "When" the tunnel repairs might be carried out, and at what cost. Due to the severity of the blaze and possible geological damage, the repair time factor proved difficult to estimate. Some thought only a matter of weeks, most opted for three-months. In point of fact from the outbreak of the fire to being opened as a fully operational rail tunnel, eight-months were to elapse. As to the cost, BR's original estimate of £950,000 was close, they finally picked up a bill of £1 million.

The first task of restoration was to relay a quarter-mile of track, which included replacement of ballast. Repairs to the tunnel cavity although extensive proved relatively straight-forward in execution; after cleaning the brickwork with high-pressure hoses, steel mesh was affixed and sprayed with rapid hardening cement. The two badly damaged air shafts were however on the verge of collapse.

Prodigiously high temperatures generated as forced draught flames roared up both air shafts like blast-furnaces, causing the brick linings to shrink. Trial boreholes revealed gaps of up to 3in wide between the brickwork and surrounding rock, rendering both shafts dangerously unstable. The resultant loss of binding between rock and brickwork, had transferred the gross weight of two very deep air shafts onto the tunnel roof at points where the structure had been weakened by fire, danger of a major collapse was very real.

A novel scheme designed to overcome these problems by the use of steel bolts and anchors was agreed by BR engineers and Whitley Moran, the repair contractors. Mr Stuart Duncan, British Rail Area Engineer, commenting on the proposals said "...this is an extremely tricky job which has to be done extremely carefully". A hydraulic drilling rig was used to bore a series of holes through the shoulders of the tunnel into solid rock (32), into which tensioned steel anchors were driven. By binding the air shaft lining back to solid rock the tunnel roof was relieved of its burden, according to Mr Duncan the use of tensioned steel anchors in this way was a "first" for BR engineers. Once the two shafts had been made safe they were filled with a plastic foam and capped.

32. Hydraulic drilling rig at work in the tunnel

The aftermath of Britain's worst tunnel fire sparked off a spate of inquiries, not to apportion blame, but which sought answers to some very searching questions, in a bid to find out how it had happened. At one such inquiry it was inferred that the train crew had not been fully aware of the exact nature of the load they were transporting. Indeed, when the train guard telephoned Preston power signal-box to raise the alarm the word "petrol" was not used. In consequence the emergency services arrived at the scene of the disaster unaware of the precise nature of the fire. At first the train was thought to be carrying gas-oil. Hazard identification markings for liquid petroleum displayed on each tanker were not dissimilar from those used for gas-oil, even though petrol has a flashpoint of 21°C, compared with gas-oil at 160°C.

Understandably questions were asked as to whether the firemen, and train crew, would have re-entered the tunnel had they known the blazing train was laden with highly inflammable petrol. The answer to which was an unequivocal yes. An unswerving loyalty towards each other, and duty to those they seek to serve took the firemen into the tunnel, sheer professionalism told them when to get out.

THE OPENING CEREMONY

With only a matter of days to go before the official reopening of the tunnel the ceremony was threatened by postponement, fire had broken out in the foam used to fill the two irreparably damaged air shafts. For several days the smouldering polyurethane gave off highly toxic fumes. Fortunately the fire was extinguished allowing the ceremony to proceed as planned on 19 August 1985.

Officiating at the ceremony Malcolm Southgate, London Midland General Manager, unveiled a commemorative plaque at Todmorden railway station. In his speech Mr Southgate thanked everyone involved with the reopening of the Calder Valley line. There were many unsung heroes performing unsolicited acts of kindness on that fateful day of the great fire. Like the young ambulance cadets who cared for those evacuated from their homes, and Tony Pollard, the well-known chip shop proprietor in Walsden, who provided over 250 meals for the emergency service personnel.

Mr Southgate announced that because of its easy gradients the Calder Valley line was to be designated BRs main trans-Pennine freight artery, leaving the Diggle – Huddersfield route clear for high-speed passenger trains. Within days the merry-go-round of trains from the Yorkshire coalfields to Fiddlers Ferry Power Station were passing through Summit tunnel. The lines provincial passenger service was also upgraded with a mixture of Sprinter 150s and Railbuses.

33. *The tunnel reopening celebrations began by unveiling a plaque and breaking a commemorative tape at Todmorden railway station, August 1985*

The two official trains, brand new 141/143 Eastern Region diesel multiple units, carried a full compliment of VIPs including; Local government representatives, Greater Manchester & West Yorkshire PTE, Local MPs, and the contractors agents. A commemorative tape was broken at Todmorden railway station (33) before proceeding through the refurbished tunnel. At Smithybridge the trains stopped to officially open its brand-new station; a £100,000 unstaffed halt paid for by the Greater Manchester Council, as part of its urban renewal programme (34 & 35).

History it is said has a habit of repeating itself, sometimes twice. It was a fitting analogy that, as in 1841 when a goods train made the maiden transit of the newly opened tunnel, so it was in 1985. After the reopening celebrations had been concluded the first train to pass through Summit tunnel was the 02.22am Manchester Victoria – Bradford newspaper service. Also, as in 1839 when rail passengers were carried forward from Littleborough station by horse-drawn carriages into Yorkshire, 146 years later during repairs to the fire ravaged tunnel Metro double-decker buses of West Yorkshire PTE operated an identical service through the Summit Pass.

PAST

AND

PRESENT

34. *First station-master at Smithybridge appointed 1868*

35. *Smithybridge railway station officially reopened as an unstaffed halt August 1985*

POSTSCRIPT

Many people will be saddened to read comments made during the aftermath of the tunnel fire, regarding bus conveyed rail passengers contemplating the Summit Pass for the first time. In his book *The Railways of Britain* Jack Simmonds describes the Pass as being "...the wild and gloomy moorland pass beneath which the tunnel was built". Perhaps Professor Simmonds made his journey when the winding Pass wore its winter mantle, for if in all truth the Summit Pass cannot be described as awe-inspiring, it is most certainly not gloomy, nor can it be described as moorland in character.

A group of American railway buffs who became interested in the Summit tunnel after reading *World From Rough Stones,* a novel by Malcolm MacDonald loosely based on the building of the Pennine bore, visited Summit to inspect the tunnel after the fire.

A summer of events entitled "Summit 150" to celebrate the 150th anniversary of the building of Summit tunnel began in style on 1 March 1991. A Sprinter train passing through the tunnel spearheaded the festivities. On board was the Patron of Summit 150 Colin Welland, actor /playwright – a keen railway enthusiast, VIPs, civic dignitaries, the gallant crew of the illfated tanker train involved in the tunnel fire, and descendants of the Stephenson family – G S would have approved.

AUTHOR'S NOTES AND ACKNOWLEDGMENTS

Ever mindful of a remark made by a late relative of mine who once said; "...More lies appear in print than by any other agency through which knowledge is imparted", I have exercised the utmost care correlating all the historical data included in this work. Whilst making no pretensions towards infallibility, it is as true and accurate account of bygone events as records permit. Research has revealed the late avuncular Cassandra of my family circle was not all that far-out with his contentious utterance. Save that is, for want of better understanding, the word disinformation would have been more appropriate, rather than accuse all scribes of half-truths or deliberate untruths.

I am indebted to Mr A H King and his assistant Mr G McLean of British Rail for granting lineside permits, and their generosity in supplying BR drawings and specifications of the Summit tunnel contracts, which are now deposited at the Rochdale Local Studies Library, along with my research papers.

My thanks to the staff Public Record Office, Kew, London, for their assistance with the voluminous M&L Rly. Co. papers. Also, the Science Museum, Geological Society of London, and Mr S K Ellison, Archivist at the House of Lords Record Office. To J E Shelbourn, general secretary of the Transport Ticket Society, for the photograph of a rare Edmondson railway ticket. David G Geldard, Michael G D Farr, Dr Richard L Hills MA PhD DIC John Marshall, John Cole, Alan Jones, and Henry R Holt, the famous brick collector of Rossendale, for their valued help. The proprietors of G & N Scott Ltd. Drake Street, Rochdale, for kind permission to reproduce newspaper photographs. Also, UMIST, The Museum of Science & Industry, Manchester, Littleborough Historical Society, and Roman Photographics, Mexborough, South Yorkshire.

I am grateful to Pam Godman and her staff at Rochdale Local Studies Library, for their help. Also the staff of Reference Libraries in; Halifax, Lancaster, Leeds, London, Manchester, Oldham, Preston, Rotherham, Todmorden, and Wigan, for their help in providing photographs, photostatic copies of newspaper reports, and other relevant material. A special thanks, of course, to my publisher George Kelsall.

Finally, I wish to record my sincere thanks to Peter for typing the text from my chaotic manuscript, and Paul for his technical assistance with the production of a printer's draft.

Rochdale   **A H**

BIBLIOGRAPHY

NEWSPAPERS AND JOURNALS

Bradford Observer, 1843

British Rail, Summit tunnel Barco Neg drawings and contractors specifications, 1837

Civil Engineers & Architects Journal, 1840

Halifax Courier & Guardian, 1840 & 1882

Halifax Evening Courier, 1982

Herapaths Railway Magazine, 1839

Illustrated London News, 1845

Journal of Transport History, 1973 & 1975

Leeds Mercury, 1840

Manchester Guardian, 1837-41

Min. Proc. *The Institute of Civil Engineers*,vol 72, pp 300-8 1883

Railway Magazine, 1905

Railway Times, 1838-42

Rochdale Observer, 1984-5

BOOKS AND PAMPHLETS

A Companion to the Manchester & Leeds Railway, Nicholson & Wilson, Halifax 1841

Ahrons, E L, *The British Steam Locomotive 1825 – 1925*, Ian Allen Ltd. 1927

Bairstow, M, *The Manchester & Leeds Railway*, author, Halifax, 1987

Barret, Revd D W, *Life and Work among the Railway Navvies*, Wills & Gardener, London 1880

Beaver, P, *A History of Tunnelling*, 1972

Blakemore, M, *The Lancashire & Yorkshire Railway*, Ian Allen Ltd. 1984

Brees, S C, *Railway Practice*, 5 vols, John Williams, London 1838

Butterworth, E, *An Historical Sketch of the Manchester & Leeds Railway as far as completed*, E Wrigley, Rochdale 1839

Coleman, T, *The Railway Navvies*, 1963 (republished Penguin pb 1981)

Condor, F R, *Personal Recollections of English Engineers*, Hodder & Stoughton, 1868

Farr, M G D, *Thomas Edmondson Transport Ticket Pioneer*, author 1979

Francis, J A, *A History of the English Railway 1820-45*, 2 vols, Longman 1851 (reprinted Augustus M Kelly, New York 1968)

Gooch, Sir D, *Memoirs and Diary*, author,

Kegan Paul, Trench Trubner & Co. Ltd. 1892 (republished under new title 1972)

Jackson, F, *Snapshots of Littleborough*, author, 1943

Lecount, Lieutenant P A, *A Practical Treatise on Railways*, A & C Black, Edinburgh 1839

Marshall, J, *The Lancashire & Yorkshire Railway*, 3 vols, David & Charles, Newton Abbot 1969-72

Normington, T, *The Lancashire & Yorkshire Railway*, Manchester 1898

Parry, K, *Survivor! The Summit Tunnel*, author, 1985

Rolt, L T C, *George and Robert Stephenson*, Longman 1960

Sandstrom, Gosta E, *The History of Tunnelling*, 1963

Simmonds, J, *The Railways of Britain*, Macmillan, London 1986

Smiles, S, *Lives of the Engineers George and Robert Stephenson*, Murray, London 1904

Summerside, T, *Anecdotes, Reminiscences and Conversations of and with the late George Stephenson, Father of Railways*, author, London 1878

Snell, S, *The Story of Railway Pioneers*, Selwyn & Blount Ltd. London 1921

Tait, A F, *Views on the Manchester and Leeds Railway – twenty lithographs*, text by E Butterworth, Bradshaw & Blacklock, Manchster 1845

Taylor, Rebe P, *Rochdale Retrospect*, Corporation of Rochdale, 1956

Travis, J, *Historical and Personal Notes upon the Village of Littleborough*, Chambers, Todmorden 1890 (reprinted 1984)

Whishaw, F, *Analysis of Railways*, Weale, High Holborn

Whishaw, F, *Railways of Great Britain and Ireland*, 1842 (reprinted 1969)

Williams, F S, *Our Iron Roads*, Ingram Cooke, London 1852

Williams, F S, *The Midland Railway its Rise and Progress*, Straham & Co. 1876

Wood, N, *A Practical Treatise of Railroads*, London 1825